ELIAS BOUDINOT, CHEROKEE
AND HIS AMERICA

THE CIVILIZATION OF THE AMERICAN INDIAN

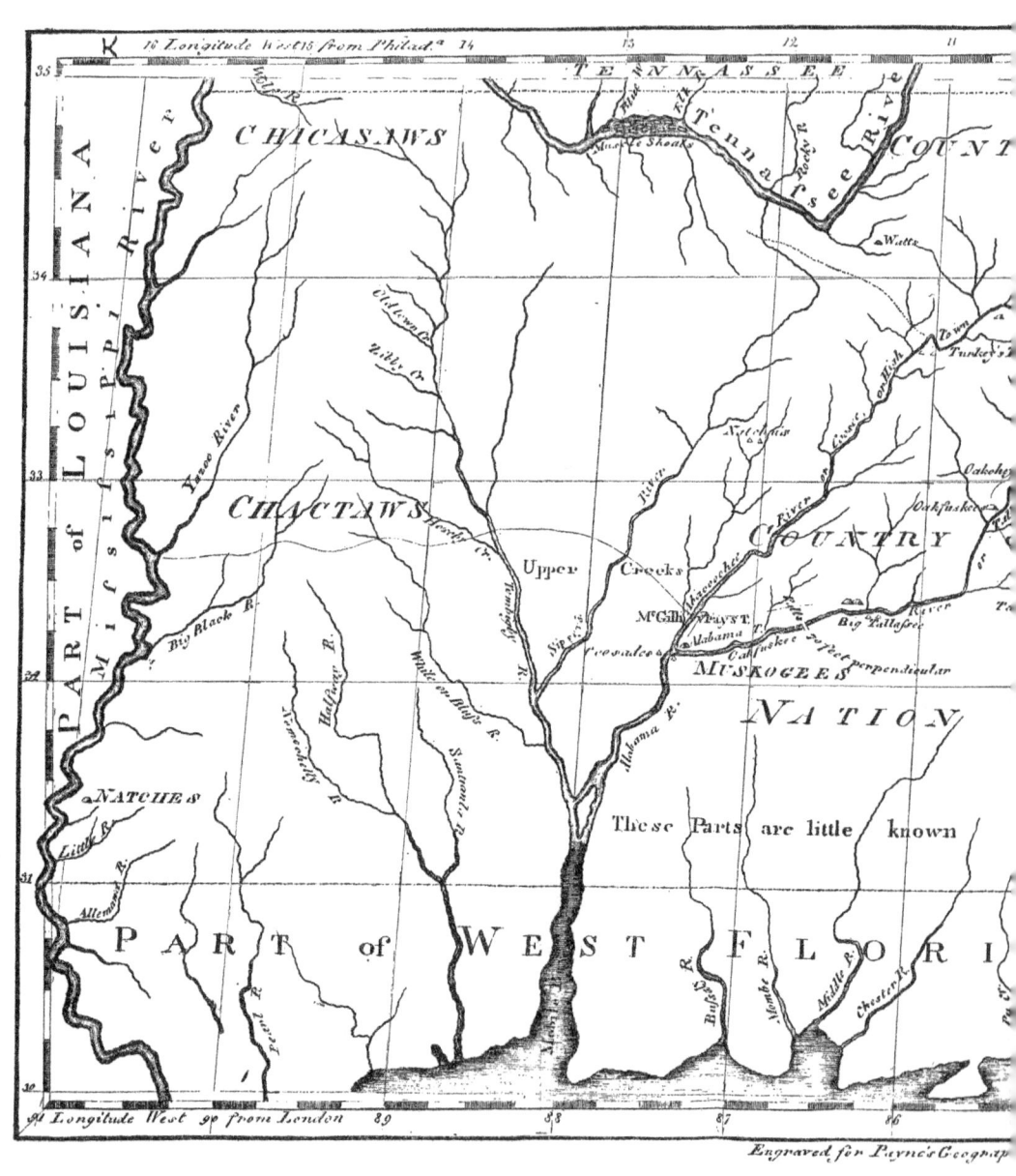

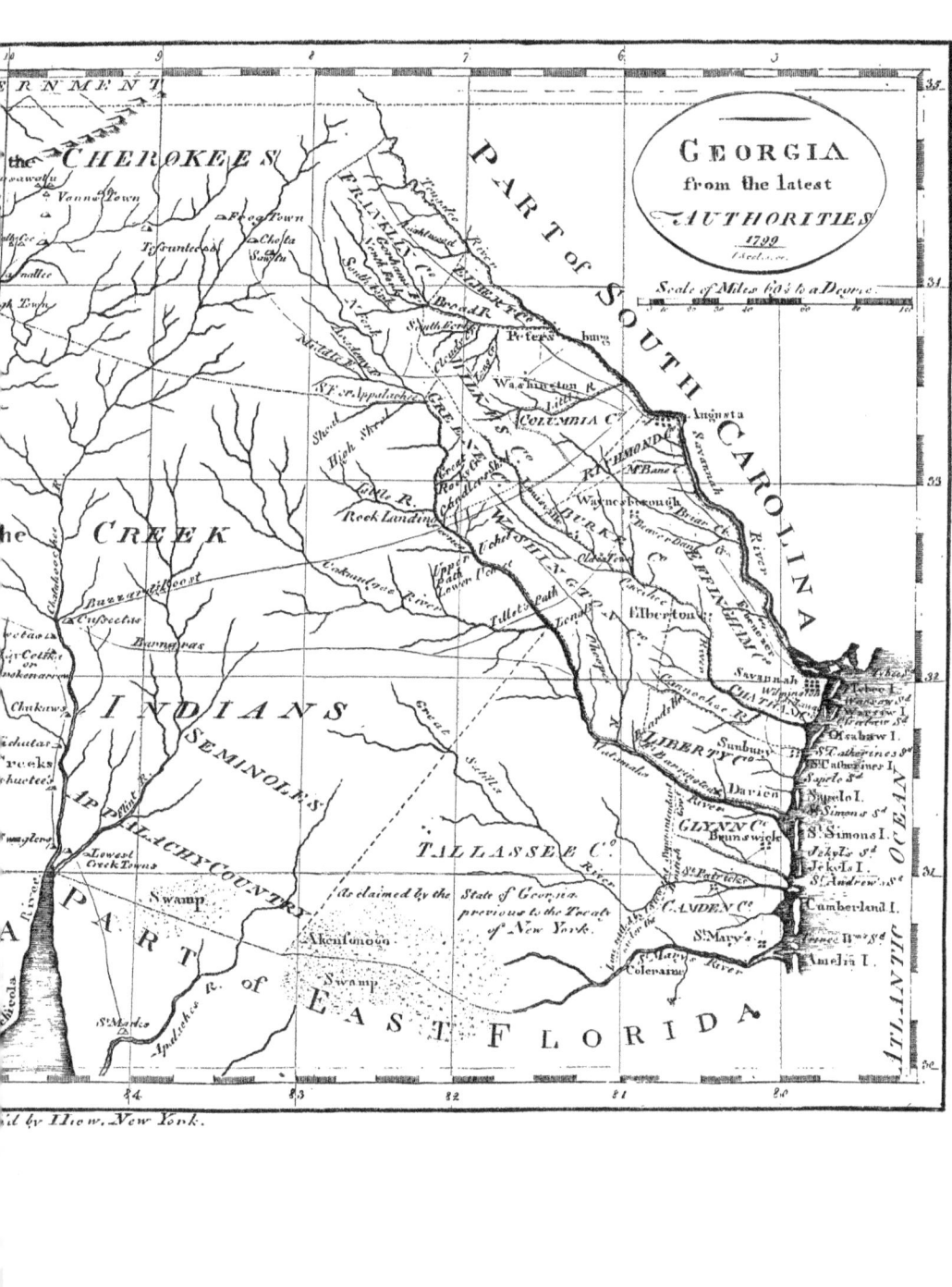

Elias Boudinot
From an oil portrait; artist unknown

ELIAS BOUDINOT
Cherokee
&
HIS AMERICA

By
RALPH HENRY GABRIEL

NORMAN
UNIVERSITY OF OKLAHOMA PRESS
1941

For
Alta Monroe Gabriel
and
the memory of
Er Cleveland Gabriel

Copyright 1941
BY THE
UNIVERSITY OF OKLAHOMA PRESS
ALL RIGHTS RESERVED

SET UP AND PRINTED IN THE UNITED STATES
BY THE UNIVERSITY OF OKLAHOMA PRESS
PUBLISHING DIVISION OF THE
UNIVERSITY

First Edition, 1941

ᏣᎳᎩ ᏧᎴᎯᏌᏅᎯ

CHEROKEE PHŒNIX.

VOL. I. NEW ECHOTA, THURSDAY MARCH 13, 1828. **NO. 4.**

EDITED BY ELIAS BOUDINOTT.
PRINTED WEEKLY BY
ISAAC H. HARRIS,
FOR THE CHEROKEE NATION.

At $2 50 if paid in advance, $3 in six months, or $3 50 if paid at the end of the year.

To subscribers who can read only the Cherokee language the price will be $2,00 in advance, or $2,50 to be paid within the year.

Every subscription will be considered as continued unless subscribers give notice to the contrary before the commencement of a new year.

The Phœnix will be printed on a Super-Royal sheet, with type entirely new procured for the purpose. Any person procuring six subscribers, and becoming responsible for the payment, shall receive a seventh gratis.

Advertisements will be inserted at seventy-five cents per square for the first insertion, and thirty-seven and a half cents for each continuance; longer ones in proportion.

☞ All letters addressed to the Editor, post paid, will receive due attention.

CHEROKEE LAWS.

The following laws of the Cherokee Nation we publish as we find them in print, and we presume may be typographical errors. They have already been introduced to this Nation in a pamphlet form.—Our readers at a distance will perhaps be gratified to note the first commencement of written laws among the Cherokees. We publish some that are not now in force. The repealing laws will appear in the order in which they were passed.

LAWS.

Resolved by the Chiefs and Warriors in a national council assembled, That it shall be, and is hereby authorized, for regulating parties to be organized to consist of six men in each company; one captain, one lieutenant and four privates, to continue in service for the term of one year, whose duties it shall be to suppress horse stealing and the robbery of other property within their respective bounds, who shall be paid out of the national annuity, at the rates of fifty dollars to each captain, forty to the lieutenant, and thirty dollars to each of the privates; and to give their protection to children as heirs to their fathers' property, and to the widow's share whom he may have had children by, or cohabited with, as his wife, at the time of his decease; and in case a father shall leave or will any property to a child at the time of his decease which he may have had by another woman, then, his present wife shall be entitled to receive any such property as may be left by him as above, when substantiated by one or two disinterested witnesses.

Be it resolved by the Council aforesaid, When any person or persons which may or shall be charged with stealing a horse and upon conviction by one or two witnesses, he, she or they shall be punished with one hundred stripes on the bare back, and the punishment be in proportion for stealing property of less value; and should the accused person or persons rise up with arms in his or their hands, as guns, axes, spears and knives, in opposition to the regulating company, and should they kill him or them, the blood of him or them shall not be required of any of the persons belonging to the regulators from the clan the person so killed belonged to.

Accepted,
BLACK FOX, Principal Chief.
PATH KILLER, Seco'l.
TOOCHALAR.
CHARLES HICKS, Sec'y to the Council.
Broom's Town, Sept. 11th, 1808.

Be it known, That this day, the various clans or tribes which compose the Cherokee Nation, have unanimously passed an act of oblivion for all lives for which they may have been indebted, one to the other, and have mutually agreed that after this evening the aforesaid act shall become binding upon every clan, or tribe; and the aforesaid clans or tribes have also agreed that if in future, any life should be lost without malice intended, the innocent aggressor shall not be accounted guilty.

Be it known also, That should it so happen that a brother, forgetting his natural affection, should raise his hand in anger and kill his brother, he shall be accounted guilty of murder and suffer accordingly. And if a man has a horse stolen, and overtakes the thief, and should his anger be so great as to cause him to kill him, let his blood remain on his own conscience, but no satisfaction shall be demanded for his life from his relatives or the clan he may belong to.

By order of the seven clans.
TURTLE AT HOME,
Speaker of Council.

Approved.
BLACK FOX, Principal Chief.
PATH KILLER, Seco'l.
TOOCHALAR.
CHARLES HICKS, Sec'y to the Council.
Oostanallah, April 10, 1810.

WHEREAS, fifty-four towns and villages having convened in order to deliberate and consider on the situation of our nation, in the disposition of our common property of lands without the unanimous consent of the members of the Council, and in order to divide the civil consequences resulting in such course, we have unanimously adopted the following form for the future government of our nation.

ARTICLE 1st. It is unanimously agreed, that there shall be thirteen members elected as a Standing Committee for the term of two years, at the end of which term they shall be either re-elected or others; and in consequence of the death or resignation of any of said Committee, our head Chiefs shall elect another to fill the vacancy.

ARTICLE 2d. The affairs of the Cherokee Nation shall be committed to the care of the Standing Committee: but the acts of this body shall not be binding on the Nation in our common property, without the unanimous consent of the members and Chiefs of the Council, which they shall present for their acceptance or dissent.

ARTICLE 3d. The authority and claim of our common property shall cease with the person or persons who shall think proper to remove themselves without the limits of the Cherokee Nation.

ARTICLE 4th. The improvements and labors of our people by the mother's side shall be inviolate during the time of their occupancy.

ARTICLE 5th. This Committee shall settle with the Agency for our annual stipend, and report their proceedings to the members and Chiefs in council; but the friendly communication between our head Chiefs and the Agency shall remain free and open.

ARTICLE 6th. The above articles for our government, may be amended at our electional term, and the Committee is hereby required, to be governed by the above articles; and the Chiefs and Warriors in Council unanimously pledge themselves to observe strictly the contents of the above articles.—Whereunto we have set our heads and seals at Amoah, this 6th day of May, one thousand eight hundred and seventeen.

Approved in Council, on the day and date above written.

EHNAUTAUNAUEH,
Speaker to the Council.

Approved of in the written government by the head Chief,
his
PATH ✕ KILLER,
mark.
A. McCOY, Sec'y to the Council.
CHARLES HICKS.

[TO BE CONTINUED.]

---

29 ᎦᏚᏉᏁ, 1827.

1817.

SCANDAL.

'There are people,' continued the corporal, 'who can't even breathe, without slandering a neighbor.'

'You judge too severely,' replied my aunt Prudy, 'no one is slandered who does not deserve it.'

'That may be,' retorted the corporal, 'but I have heard very slight things said of you.'

The face of my aunt kindled with anger. 'Me!' she exclaimed, 'never— sight things of me! what can any body say of me?'

'They say,' answered the corporal gravely, and drawing his words to keep her in suspense, 'that—that you keep too low company than you ought to be.'

Fury flashed from the eyes of my aunt.

'Who are the wretches?'

'I hope they slander no one who does not deserve it,' remarked the corporal jeeringly, as he left the room.

The feelings of my aunt may well be conceived. She was sensibly injured. True she had her foibles.— She was peevish and fretful. But she was rigidly moral and virtuous.— The purest sex was not more chaste. The Pope himself could not boast more piety. Conscious of the correctness of her conduct, she was wounded at the remark of the corporal. 'Why should her neighbors slander her? She could not conceive.

Let my aunt be consoled. A person who can live in this world without suffering slander, must be too stupid or insignificant to claim attention.

Cannibalism.—Extract of a letter from Messrs. Tyerman and Bennett, to Mr. Loomis, of the Sandwich Island mission, dated Eaton, Nov. 1825:

"We touched at New Zealand; and owing to the imprudence of our captain, the natives rose upon us, took us, and our vessel—tied us with their hands almost an hour and a half. They stood over us with uplifted axes and weapons of destruction, as if waiting till some signal should be given;—and we expected every moment to be our last, and to be eaten as soon as killed. One of these horrid cannibals came and handed my person to see what sort of food I should be for them. At length a boat arrived, in which was a chief of influence and ten of the Wesleyan missionaries. The chief acted the most friendly part, as well as the missionary, and we were delivered and peace restored. This very chief, who came as our deliverer, had a few years before instigated a plot, and out of a large ship, and the whole crew were devoured, upwards of ninety persons. The wreck of this ship was before our eyes at the moment of our captivity."

A Letter

Mr. Dudley L. Vaill,
 Winsted, Connecticut.

DEAR MR. VAILL:

The sheaf of letters which you generously put at my disposal makes it possible to reconstruct a story known before only in outline. The principals in the narrative rose in their day above mediocrity. Elias Boudinot achieved sufficient fame to give him a column in the "Dictionary of American Biography," but he was, at best, a minor figure. Americans, moreover, have been glad to forget the tragedy in which his life reached its climax. In writing his biography (out of the materials you have made available and others I have gathered) my purpose has not been primarily to set forth the events of Boudinot's career. I have been interested in the changing Cherokee mind of his day—and the part he played in its evolution.

Elias Boudinot might have grown up a worshiper of the old Cherokee gods. Fate, however, made him a Puritan of the New England stamp. He married a New England girl, Harriet Gold, whose rare strength of character was an aid to him as long as she lived. The outlook and standards of Harriet Gold and of her parents make clear the pattern of early nineteenth century New England Puritanism at its best. The ordeal through which this family passed after the announcement of a proposed marriage across the race line displays that same Puritanism at its worst. My purpose has been to write the biography of Harriet Gold as well as that of Elias Boudinot, but again my objective has been to discover the mind of Puritan Connecticut. It was this Puritanism which Boudinot sought to carry to his people. His great decision in the fateful year, 1835, was made within a framework of Puritan thought.

But the story of this red man and white woman, drawn together by common ideals and similar religious and humanitarian motives, has value for itself. It is one of the most poignant in American history. It can be reconstructed from letters which are extraordinary for frankness and detail. I have tried, wherever possible, to let the actors in the tale speak for themselves. In no other way can our generation catch the inner thoughts of these people of another age or achieve an understanding of the climate of opinion in which they lived.

Above all else, however, this essay is a study of American Protestantism confronting not only a race problem but that of adjustment between two cultures separated by a thousand years. The following pages recount the failure of the gospel of brotherhood to triumph over the philosophy of force and of refusal of the faithful to accept defeat. The story is not without value in this twentieth century when the warfare between the philosophies of force and of brotherhood has reached world wide proportions.

Sincerely,

RALPH H. GABRIEL

Trumbull College
Yale University
January 15, 1941

Acknowledgments

MANY thanks are due the American Board of Commissioners of Foreign Missions and the librarian of the Andover Theological Seminary for permitting me to use the manuscript letters of Samuel Worcester. I am grateful to staffs of the Bureau of Indian Affairs, the Congressional Library, and the Sterling Memorial Library at Yale for valuable aid and coöperation. To Professor Edward E. Dale of the University of Oklahoma I am indebted for suggestions in the earlier stages of this work. My colleagues, Professors Alfred Bellinger, Sydney K. Mitchell, and the late Ulrich B. Phillips, have generously assisted me by reading portions of the manuscript. Dr. Charles R. Keller of Williams College and Dr. Charles M. Andrews have read the entire manuscript and have given help. The section of the narrative which deals with the Cherokees has been read by Mr. Frank J. Boudinot, who has also very kindly supplied photographs of his grandparents, Elias and Harriet Gold Boudinot. Miss Lilian Gold assisted in an attempt to identify the artist who painted the portraits. Mr. Savoie Lottinville, Director of the University of Oklahoma Press, has made many valuable suggestions and has given generous assistance. Without the coöperation of Mr. Dudley L. Vaill, who possesses the letters, the work could never have been begun.

R. H. G.

Table of Contents

	A LETTER	ix
	ACKNOWLEDGMENTS	xi

Part I. The Southern Appalachians

I.	THE GREAT BUZZARD	3
II.	NATURE	15
III.	SPRING PLACE	22

Part II. The Litchfield Hills

IV.	OBOOKIAH	33
V.	BENJAMIN GOLD	43
VI.	THE FOREIGN MISSION SCHOOL	49
VII.	ISAIAH BUNCE	57
VIII.	FIGHTING AGAINST GOD	66
IX.	THE SMOKE OF THEIR TORMENT	73
X.	THE TRIBE OF GOLD	81
XI.	DAWN	89

Part III. Brotherhood or Force

XII.	HIGH TOWER	95
XIII.	SEQUOYAH	101
XIV.	A PRESS FOR THE CHEROKEES	106

XV.	NEW ECHOTA	111
XVI.	THE WHITE TERROR	120
XVII.	PRISON	128
XVIII.	JOHN ROSS	134
XIX.	RED CLAY	141
XX.	A QUESTION OF ETHICS	148
XXI.	HARRIET	156
XXII.	A HUMBLE INDIVIDUAL	159
XXIII.	THE TRAIL OF TEARS	165

Part IV. The West

XXIV.	THE DARKENING LAND	175
	APPENDIX	181
	INDEX	189

List of Illustrations

ELIAS BOUDINOT	FRONTISPIECE
MAP: GEORGIA IN 1799	II-III
THE CHEROKEE PHŒNIX, MARCH 13, 1828	VII
THE FOREIGN MISSION SCHOOL AT CORNWALL, CONNECTICUT	54
CORNWALL VILLAGE IN 1838, & GOSHEN, CONNECTICUT, AND THE ROAD FROM CORNWALL TO LITCHFIELD	64
HARRIET GOLD BOUDINOT	76

PART I
THE SOUTHERN APPALACHIANS

1

The Great Buzzard

~~~

MAY 26, 1826, found many carriages stopping before the door of the First Presbyterian Church of Philadelphia. The respectability and aristocracy of the city alighted and betook themselves to familiar pews with much rustling of crinoline and nodding to acquaintances. Doubtless many of the audience were accustomed to repair to this place from time to time to listen to addresses upon one or another of the many new methods being proposed for the uplifting of mankind. The humanitarian movement of the first half of the nineteenth century was in full swing. It stemmed from the humanism of the eighteenth century Enlightenment and from a quickened Puritanism which, under the preaching of Timothy Dwight, grandson of Jonathan Edwards, was undergoing a renaissance. Both east and west of the Appalachians American evangelical Protestantism was advancing. Church members were leaders in the movement for social reform on every humanitarian front.

On May 26, the Philadelphians gathered for no ordinary occasion. On this day the familiar subjects of temperance and slavery were laid aside. With curiosity and anticipation the audience prepared to listen to an Indian, direct from the wilds. He bore the name of New Jersey's most celebrated philanthropist who but a few years before had passed to his reward. The assembled humanitarians stirred as Elias Boudinot stood before them. He was handsome and well formed, and he looked, even in the conventional dress of the white man, every inch the Indian.

For Boudinot the meeting meant something quite different from a pleasant thrill. The copper-colored son of the southern Appalachians felt a heavy responsibility. Through him a people who knew practically nothing of the world beyond the azalea-covered slopes of their uplands was addressing the heart and the conscience of America. Boudinot knew that his words would not die within the four walls of the auditorium but were to be broadcast in a pamphlet over the imprint of the First Church.

"What is an Indian?" Boudinot asked quietly. "Is he not formed of the same materials with yourself? ... You here behold an Indian, my kindred are Indians, and my fathers sleeping in the wilderness grave—they too were Indians. But I am not as my fathers were—broader means and nobler influences have fallen upon me. ... In a lonely cabin, overspread by the forest oak, I first drew my breath; and in a language unknown to learned and polished nations, I learnt ... my ... mother's name. In after days I have had greater advantages than most of my race; and I now stand before you delegated by my native country to seek her interest, to labour for her respectability, and by my public efforts to assist in raising her to an equal standing with other nations of the earth. ..."

Boudinot, as he spoke in Philadelphia, was approaching the zenith of his career. Behind him was the story of an Indian boy plucked by missionaries from a mountain hut who made the long journey to New England to study in a school in Connecticut and in the Andover Theological

Seminary. Before him stretched years of service to his nation and his race, threatened with disaster.

The Unakas and the Great Smokies dominate the uplands of the southern Appalachians where ridges contend with ridges like the waves of a stormy sea. From Clingman's Dome stretches as far as the eye can reach a tumbled wilderness where mountains seem to be piled on mountains and rivers gleam in the valleys. The chaos of the southern Appalachians and the country immediately about their base on the south and west were the ancient tribal home of the Cherokees.

They knew well the forest extending from the lowlands almost to the mountain tops. Magnolias, pawpaws, persimmons, and mulberries were massed on the lower slopes of the great domes like an army preparing for an advance. Part way up the sides the southern trees were joined by reinforcements of maples, oaks, hickories, and beeches. Farther on the van was led by the birches, spruces, and balsams of the north. But even these hardy species, familiar with cold and snow, failed to gain many a summit, and a bald knob rose above the mantle of vegetation. Deer fed in the forest, and bears wallowed in the swamps which formed in the hollows of the mountain sides. Wild turkeys fattened on the fruit of the underbrush; ravens croaked in the tree tops; and silent buzzards circled among the domes.

The Cherokees, looking up to the ridges from their towns in the valleys, recalled an old story which explained the making of their mountains. These peaks were raised when the earth was still but a flat and muddy island in a great sea and before the sun had been put in the skyvault to dry it. The animals who then lived in a land beyond the skyvault were anxious to learn whether the new earth were yet ready for them to live on. They sent the Great Buzzard, the father of all buzzards, to look for a dry spot. He winged his solitary way over the expanse of mud so long that he grew weary. He flew lower and lower, and his huge, flapping wings began to strike the earth. Wherever they struck, a valley appeared, and where they turned up again there was a mountain. When the animals above saw what was happening, they were afraid that the whole world would be rough and broken country, so they called back the Great Buzzard. But the Cherokee country remains full of mountains to this day.[1]

In ancient days when they were undisputed masters of their uplands, the Cherokees were hunters with stone-tipped spears and arrows. The abundant game of the forest offered an adequate food supply. The women contributed their share to the sustenance of the villages by gardening on the rich and well-watered soil of the valley bottoms. Protected by their stony ramparts from annihilating attack, the Cherokees prospered. They increased in number until they probably surpassed the population of their northern kinsmen, the Iroquois. In the second quarter of the eighteenth century their towns were estimated to contain twenty thousand people, and their six thousand warriors made them one of the most powerful tribes within the boundaries of what is now the United States.

In the first year of the American Revolution a botanist from Pennsylvania, William Bartram, more interested in the vegetable kingdom than in that of George III, pene-

---

[1] James Mooney, "Myths of the Cherokee," *Nineteenth Annual Report*, Bureau of American Ethnology, Part I, 239.

trated the Cherokee mountains in search of new plants for his herbarium. The Indians received him with courtesy and made his stay pleasant. When he returned to his own country, he described them with frank admiration. "The women of the Cherokees," he commented, "are tall, slender, erect and of delicate frame, their features formed of a perfect symmetry, their countenance cheerful and friendly, and they move with a becoming grace and dignity. ... The Cherokees in their dispositions and manners are grave and steady; dignified and circumspect in their deportment; rather slow and reserved in conversation; yet frank, cheerful and humane; tenacious of their liberties and the natural rights of men; secret, deliberative and determined in their councils; honest, just and liberal and are ready always to sacrifice every pleasure and gratification, even their blood, and life itself, to defend their territory and maintain their rights."[2]

The enthusiastic young Bartram came near mistaking the Cherokee brave for Rousseau's noble savage. The white borderers of the frontier, through which he passed on his way to and from the uplands, felt differently about their red neighbors. These leather-shirted riflemen saw in the mountain Indians only fierce and treacherous savages who balked the white man's efforts to get more land.

The Cherokees lived in large towns, picturesque aggregations of cabins sprawling without pattern along the bank of a river.[3] Individual habitations were made of logs, the chinks well plastered with clay tempered with grass to keep

[2] William Bartram, *Travels* ... (London, reprinted for J. Johnson, 1792), 481-3.
[3] For the following description of the Cherokees I have depended primarily upon James Adair, *The History of the American Indians* ... (London, printed for E. C. Dilly, 1775).

out the winds of the cold months. Near each cabin was a small conical structure where the whole family slept beside a slow fire on winter nights. In spite of the cold of their country the Cherokees wore little clothing. An ancient religious custom sent them to the river at dawn each day even in freezing weather for a ceremonial plunge to wash away their impurities. As they returned from the water's edge singing chants, they could see the morning sun lighting the bark on the conical roof of the council house which, like a cathedral, dominated the village. It stood on a mound in the midst of the town. A single door opened upon a dim interior where hundreds of persons could sit. It was lighted at night by blazing lightwood.

The townhouse was the political, social, and ceremonial center of the village and symbolized the unity of the village group. The Cherokee Nation up to the end of the eighteenth century was, in fact, little more than a loose federation of towns.

In one of these, Cowe by name, William Bartram one summer night in 1775 made his way with the rest of the people to the townhouse to witness a dance. He looked curiously at the assembling audience. The women were dressed in their beads and finery, and the younger ones showed evidence of a liberal use of bear's grease to anoint the face and body. Bear's grease also kept the hair of the men sleek and shiny. The fire leaped high, lighting fitfully a mass of bronzed faces. Near it sat the musicians with their drums. The dance was in preparation for a game of ball-play or lacrosse to be held on the following day with a neighboring town. An old chief rose and delivered a long oration in commendation of the manly exercise of ball-play, not forgetting to recite his own exploits and those of the other aged men who were present. Then the drums began. "Presently a company of girls, hand in hand, dressed in clean white robes and ornamented with beads, bracelets, and a profusion of gay ribbands, entering the door, immediately began to sing their responses in a gentle, low and sweet voice, and formed themselves in a semicircular file or line, in two ranks back to back, facing the spectators and the musicians, moving slowly round and round; this continued about a quarter of an hour, when we were surprised by a sudden very loud and shrill whoop, uttered at once by a company of young fellows, who came in briskly after one another, with rackets or hurls in one hand. These champions likewise were well dressed, painted and ornamented with silver bracelets, gorgets and wampum ... moccasins and high waving plumes in their diadems, who immediately formed themselves in a semicircular rank also, in front of the girls, when these changed their order, and formed a single rank parallel to the men, raising their voices in response to the tunes of the young champions, the semicircles continually moving round. There was something singular and diverting in their step and motions. ... the movements were managed with inconceivable alertness and address, and accompanied with an instantaneous and universal elevation of the voice and shrill short whoop."

"The Cherokees," Bartram added, "besides the ball-play dance, have a variety of others equally entertaining; the men especially exercise themselves with a variety of gesticulations and capers, some of which are ludicrous and diverting enough; and they have others which are of the martial order, and others of the chase; wherein they exhibit astonishing feats of military prowess, masculine strength and activity. Indeed all their dances and musical entertainments seem to be theatrical exhibitions or plays, varied with comic and sometimes lascivious interludes; the women, however, conduct themselves with a very becoming grace and decency, insomuch that in amorous interludes, when their responses and gestures seem consenting to natural liberties, they veil themselves (with their mantles), just discovering a glance of their sparkling eyes and blushing faces, expressive of sensibility."[4]

The artificialities and restraints of eighteenth century white society contrasted strangely with the scene at Cowe. In the mountains Bartram had found an unsophisticated nature people, creatures of the forest about them. Grandfathers of Elias Boudinot had doubtless shouted and sung in many a ball-play dance like that at Cowe.

William Bartram was only a transient visitor among the Cherokees and so was not able to penetrate beneath the surface of what he saw. But James Adair knew the Cherokees thoroughly. Forty years this Scotchman spent trading with the tribes of the Old Southwest. In the very year of Bartram's excursion into the southern Appalachians Adair published in a book what he knew of his Indian friends and neighbors. He saw the culture of the Cherokees undergoing decline. "The Cheerake are now a nest of apostate hornets, pay little respect to grey hairs, and have been degenerating fast from their primitive religious principles, for above thirty years past."[5] The authority of the ancient tribal customs concerning marriage had grown perceptibly weaker, and the antagonistic Adair noted bluntly that "marriages are commonly of short duration in that wanton female gov-

---

[4] Bartram, *Travels*, 367-9.
[5] Adair, *History of the American Indians*, 81.

ernment."⁶ Contact with the whites caused the Cherokee decline. The independent hunter, without realizing it, was becoming the hired man of the trader. The arts of the stone age were disappearing as steel knives replaced those of flint, and copper kettles supplanted jars of clay.

About 1738 intercourse with the white settlements brought disaster to the Cherokees when a scourge of smallpox destroyed nearly half the nation. The shamans attributed the epidemic to the displeasure of the spirits at the adulterous conduct of the young married people. "Immediately," narrated Adair, the medicine men "ordered the reputed sinners to lie out of doors, day and night, with their breasts frequently open to the night dews, to cool the fever; they were likewise afraid that the diseased would otherwise pollute the house. ... Instead of applying warm remedies, they at last in every visit poured cold water on their naked breasts, sung their religious mystical song Yo Yo ... with a doleful tune and shaked a calabash with pebble-stones, over the sick, using a great many frantic gestures, by way of incantation. ... When they found their theological regimen had not the desired effect, but that the infection gained upon them, they held a second consultation, and deemed it the best method to sweat their patients, and plunge them into the river—which was accordingly done. Their rivers being very cold in summer by reason of the numberless springs ... [the patients] immediately expired: upon which the ... [shamans] broke their old consecrated physic-pots, and threw away all the pretended holy things they had for physical use, imagining they had lost their divine power by being polluted."⁷

⁶ *Ibid.*, 126 f.
⁷ *Ibid.*, 232 f.

The unexpected defeat of the shamans was a tragedy. They were skilled in the use of herbs, and Adair himself avowed more faith in their remedies than in those of the physicians of the white settlements. Inevitably the unchecked ravages of the smallpox impaired the prestige of these "old beloved men." Among the Cherokees a new skepticism corroded the ancient sanctions which governed conduct. Religion declined. The Cherokees began to forget the migration myth of the tribe.

Religion, however, is one of the toughest of human institutions and one not to be overthrown by a single buffeting. Though impaired in strength, the Cherokee faith persisted —these Indians had no other explanation for the mysteries about them. Thus each summer, when the corn reached maturity, the Cherokees continued to perform their most elaborate and important ritual, the Green Corn Dance, a ceremony of expiation and purification, a symbolical starting of life afresh. It was their substitute for the Christian's Easter. The dance was celebrated in many towns, but the greatest performance was that at Echota on the Tennessee River, the one sacred town of refuge of the Cherokees. The ritual continued for eight days. The homes of the people and the townhouse were swept clean. A powerful emetic was brewed and taken. The utensils of the old year were broken and thrown away. The old fires were put out. The Cherokees, rubbing themselves with the ashes of the old year, completed their purification by bathing in the river. Then new garments were put on. The fire maker, using friction, called new fire from the spirit world. Then the green corn was eaten in a gay feast. The new year had begun.

The Green Corn Dance affords the best glimpse into the

minds of the ancient hunting Cherokees. Adair has left a description of the dance which marked the climax of the festival. "While their sanctified new fruits are dressing, a religious attendant is ordered to call six of their old beloved women to come to the temple, and dance the beloved dance with joyful hearts, according to the old beloved speech. They cheerfully obey, and enter the supposed holy ground in solemn procession, each carrying in her hand a bundle of small branches of various green trees; and they join the same number of old magi, or priests, who carry a cane in one hand adorned with white feathers, having likewise green boughs in their other hand, which they pulled from their holy arbor, and carefully place there, encircling it with several rounds. Those beloved men have their heads dressed with white plumes; but the women are decked in their finest, and anointed with bear's-grease, having small tortoise-shells, and white pebbles, fastened to a piece of white-drest deer-skin, which is tied to each of their legs.

"The eldest of the priests leads the sacred dance, a-head of the innermost row, which of course is next the holy fire, by invoking *Yah,* after their usual manner, on a bass key, and with a short accent; then he sings *Yo Yo,* which is repeated by the rest of the religious procession; and he continues his sacred invocations and praises, repeating the divine word, or notes, till they return to the same point of the circular course, where they began: the *He He* in like manner, and *Wah Wah.* While dancing they never fail to repeat those notes ... with great earnestness and fervor, till they encircle the altar, while each strikes the ground with right and left feet alternately, very quick, but well-timed. Then the awful drums join the sacred choir, which incite the old female singers to chant forth their pious notes, and grateful praises before the divine essence, and to redouble their former quick joyful steps, in imitation of the leader of the sacred dance, and the religious men a-head of them. What with the manly strong notes of one, and the shrill voices of the other, in concert with the bead-shells, and the two sounding, drum-like earthen vessels, with the voices of the musicians who beat them, the ... holy ground echoes with the praises of *Yo He Wah*."[8]

[8] *Ibid.*, 96 f.

2

Nature

THE Cherokees worshiped nature; and so did William Bartram, botanist. Perhaps this fact will help to account for his undisguised liking for his mountain friends. But he and they followed different roads to the sanctuaries of their nature deities. Bartram's faith was the creation of an age that sought to free itself from the terrors and superstitions of an outworn theology. William Bartram rejected the incomprehensible God of the New England Puritans. He worshipped the Author of Nature, who had called into being the universe and had set it running according to the manner prescribed by natural law. In nature and in the hearts of men, rather than in an inspired book, Bartram found the Divine Mind revealed. Isaac Newton and Benjamin Franklin were prophets of the divinity to whom he looked for inspiration. His own task of gathering, classifying, and preserving new plants was fundamentally religious. In the azaleas and rhododendrons which flamed on the sides of the Cherokee mountains he believed he could read the thoughts of God.

The Cherokee man worshiped nature because he could not understand its mysteries and because he believed such worship had an immediate bearing on good and bad luck. It was an interesting world, this world of spirits created by the imagination of the Cherokees. It helps the explorer of the Cherokee mind to chart his course. It provides a background for the Christianity of Elias Boudinot.

"In the old days," ran the opening words of the myth which explained the origin of disease and medicine, "the beasts, birds, fishes, insects, and plants could all talk, and they and the people lived together in peace and friendship." But the people invented weapons and began to kill the animals. Therefore the latter, after holding many councils, invented diseases. When the Cherokee hunter killed a deer, he must beg his pardon; otherwise the spirit of the animal, the Little Deer, would follow the man to his house and strike him with rheumatism. Many of the plants were friendly to man. They furnished cures for the diseases which the revengeful animals sent. When the doctor was uncertain what plant to use to aid the sick man, the spirit of the plant told him.[1]

In caves in the sides of their mountains lived the Little People, the fairies of the Cherokees. They were handsome fellows, scarcely the height of a man's knee, who loved music and who spent half their time drumming and dancing. When they chose, they could accomplish great feats of magic. They were kindly and often cared for children who had strayed away from their parents. On the balds far above the caves of the Little People, the Immortals, the spirit "people who live anywhere," built their town houses. They were invisible save when they wished to be seen, and then they looked like other Indians. They too were fond of music and dancing, and many a hunter in the mountains told of hearing their dance songs and their drumming in

[1] The following myths have been selected from Mooney's definitive collection: the origin of disease. 250 ff.; the Little People, 252 ff.; the Immortals, 330 ff.; the daughter of the Sun, 252 ff.; the Rabbit, 270-75; the Raven Mockers, 401.

some invisible townhouse. The Immortals were a friendly race, as were the Little People, and often guided lost Indians home. More than once, when the Cherokees were hard pressed in battle, the Immortals had sent warriors to bring them victory. In the Little People and the Immortals the Cherokees unconsciously created symbols not only of their love for their mountains but of their sense of dependence upon the uplands.

The Sun lived on the other side of the sky vault but her daughter lived in the middle of the sky, directly over the earth. Every day in the long ago as the Sun climbed along the sky toward the west she stopped at her daughter's house for dinner. The Sun disliked the people of the earth, whom she thought ugly because they could not look at her without screwing up their faces. She became jealous when her brother, the Moon, told her the people always smiled at him. In a rage the Sun sent down such sultry rays that hundreds of Indians died, until, in despair, the afflicted ones went to the Little People for help. These wonder workers transformed two warriors—one into a rattlesnake and the other into a giant serpent, the Uktena. The two lay in wait for the Sun before her daughter's lodge. But the rattlesnake was too eager. He struck and killed the daughter, and her soul sped to the land of ghosts, the Darkening Land. The Sun mourned in her house and it was dark for many days. Again the Indians went to the Little People. The magicians then dispatched seven men, each armed with a sourwood rod, to the Darkening Land to bring back the girl. They found her dancing in the circle. When they tapped her with the rods, she fell out of the ring. They put her in a box and closed the lid. On the way home she came to life and begged to be released. But the seven made no answer.

She pleaded that she was hungry and thirsty but to no avail. Then she called that she was being smothered and asked that the lid be a little raised. The men yielded. Suddenly they heard a sound of something fluttering. Then a redbird called on a nearby bush. The Little People were angry at the disobedience of the men in opening the lid of the box. Since then no one has been able to bring back a friend from the Darkening Land. But the redbird, daughter of the Sun, brightens the mountainsides with her color. The myth suggests the depth of the feeling of the Cherokees for the beauties of their homeland.

When darkness hid the southern mountains, witches flew abroad, most dreaded among whom were the Raven Mockers. At night when an Indian lay at the brink of death, the Raven Mockers would gather, as buzzards above a wounded deer, flying through the air in fiery shapes with arms outstretched, as though they were wings, and sparks trailing behind. They came with a rushing sound, like the noise of a strong wind. From time to time they made hoarse cries, such as a raven makes when he dives in the air. They slipped, invisible, into the house to torment the sick one until they killed him. Sometimes they lifted him from his blankets and threw him on the floor while his sorrowing family believed that he was only struggling for breath. When he was dead, the Raven Mockers, without leaving a scar, took out his heart and ate it adding to their own lives the days they took from their victim. So the Cherokees personified the terrors of nature's ultimate victory over the individual.

The myths were no mere collection of curious stories. They die, as the organism in the laboratory, when they are dissected. They represent the emotional response of an unsophisticated people to the experience of life. They give a picture of the world of the imagination in which the old hunting Cherokees dwelt. They were full of magic, of beauty, and of terror, as was also, forsooth, the religion of Jonathan Edwards. They were, however, only a partial expression of the Indian's faith. Ritual, handed down from a forgotten antiquity, enabled the redmen to cross the frontier of sense perception and to live in the world of spirits. Men and women were transformed by the rhythm of the drums as they beat hour after hour through the night beside the fire in the center of the circle of dancers. The worshipers were brought into a mystical union as they joined with the song leader in the ancient tribal chants. Although they did not know it, the religion of these Indians was as old as that which came out of Nazareth. The Cherokee chieftain whom Bartram saw blow smoke from his pipe to the north, east, south, and west was in that simple gesture venerating those basic deities of the cardinal points of the compass, the gods who hold up the world, whom the Mayas were worshiping as early as the beginning of the Christian era. Mystical religion meant as much to the Cherokee as to Edwards or Timothy Dwight. But at the time of Bartram's visit and of Adair's book the old faith was dying.

William Bartram was not granted time to pause for study of the fading nature worship of the Cherokees. He met their principal war chief and learned that the anger of the "overhill towns" at the depredations of Virginia borderers was serious. Then he bade farewell to the peaceful Cowe and turned his face toward the white frontier, taking many specimens in his herbarium.

Had Bartram remained for a twelvemonth in the southern mountains, he would have beheld nature in a mood contrasting strangely with the beauty of the wild azalea. The conflagration which had flamed up about Boston in 1775 spread, as a forest fire, to the mountains of the Cherokees. The truce between the borderers and the Indians was forgotten. Passion, born of difference of color and of culture, ruled whites and reds alike. Race war roared through the valleys of the southern Appalachians. Before the winter of 1776 had stripped the trees of leaves, Cowe was but a collection of ash heaps.

It was a familiar mood of nature. The stronger race was assailing the weaker. The Puritan said that the heart of man is so full of wickedness that the conquest of evil requires a potent blend of the love of God and the fear of Hell. The deist said that nature is fundamentally good and that man, a part of nature, will in the end achieve perfection by his own efforts. The Cherokee said that the difference between the people and the animals is that the former invented weapons with which to kill. Raid swiftly followed raid. The white frontier was driven back; Indian towns were destroyed. The borderers massacred women and children with grim satisfaction. The Cherokees danced wildly about a white boy who screamed at a blazing stake until he died. The whites were many; the Indians relatively few.

After a time the Revolutionary War burned itself out. Then the stream of borderers crossing the mountains increased to a flood. Kentucky and Tennessee grew swiftly. Americans demanded and secured tract after tract of Cherokee land. The tribe was surrounded by whites on every side save the southwest, where the Creeks still lived. War had brought misery to the defeated. The Cherokee country was dotted by heaps of stones piled up by weeping women to mark the graves of their braves. For the moment, however, the Immortals had saved the tribe. Only the inaccessibility of the mountains prevented the expulsion of the Cherokees. Then the despairing Indians buried the hatchet which had so nearly destroyed them and determined to fight no more. Meanwhile nature, working as so often through a paradox, was promising to save them.

Racial antipathy is not so much a matter of instinct as of folkways. For more than a century white traders had been living among the Cherokees. Some of these were men of character and breeding. James Adair, the greatest of them all, knew Latin and Greek. If trade brought the races into contact, nature began to cement the union. A new race of mixed bloods appeared, some of whom combined the superior qualities of both whites and reds. After the close of the eighteenth century when the long struggle between the Indians and the borderers had ended in Cherokee defeat, the mixed bloods began slowly to assume the leadership of the people. The thoughtful among them had one hope, one plan—the Cherokee must acquire the civilization of his white conqueror. On that path lay safety; all others led to the abyss.

3

Spring Place

THE trail which led from the "Cherokee" mountains to the Georgia lowlands followed for a part of the way the broad valley of the Conasauga River. The traveler on that path in the spring of 1818 would have come upon a tiny cluster of buildings standing where the trail crossed a creek which some three miles farther on flowed into the Conasauga. It was a beautiful country. Five miles to the east across the floodplain rose Cohutta Mountain, its forest-covered ridge running north and south as far as the eye could reach. A dozen miles to the west the rolling country beyond the Conasauga reached a climax in a parallel ridge, the Chatoogata Mountain. The Great Buzzard had made a particularly broad stroke with his wing when he pressed out this valley of northwestern Georgia.

Three plain buildings stood beside the creek crossing, one a tiny log cabin, the other two dwellings some eighteen by twenty feet in size and a story and a half in height. Their roofs were clapboards held in place by heavy poles, and their chimneys were made of wood lined with clay. A single partition divided each of the houses into two rooms. Here at Spring Place, Brother and Sister Gambold conducted a school and maintained a Moravian mission station. About a dozen Indian boys lodged in the cabin, recited their lessons in the room of one of the houses, and worked on the fertile forty-acre clearing. Spring Place was excited in the spring of 1818, for two of its most promising pupils, The Buck and Leonard Hicks, were graduating.[1]

❧

Spring Place was the first mission station in the Cherokee country. In 1800 the small company of Moravians at Salem, North Carolina, had reached the conclusion that the Lord desired them to take thought for the souls of the Indians. September of that year found two Moravian brothers at Tellico, the Cherokee capital, awaiting the assembling of the Indian Council. One after another the chiefs came in— Doublehead, Little Turkey, Bloody Fellow, Boot, and Glass — all clad in breech clouts and blankets. To these patriarchs of the forest the agent explained that the two Moravians desired to tell them about the Great Spirit and to teach their children reading, writing, and some of the white man's art. The Council was interested, not in the Great Spirit, but in the proposed school. They asked whether the strangers would board and clothe the children sent to them to teach. The surprised Moravians emphatically informed the Indians they could not do so much. Was it not enough to offer to teach the children gratis?

The Indian mind does not reach decisions hastily. Four times the Council deliberated during the months of September and October. In the fourth meeting Doublehead made a long speech urging that the strangers be permitted to have a trial. If their conduct was not satisfactory, the Cherokee Nation could send them out of its territory. There were other speeches. Then the Council gave its con-

---

[1] The material of this chapter was obtained from the Rev. Edmund Schwarze, *History of the Moravian Missions Among Southern Indian Tribes of the United States* (Bethlehem, Pa., Times Publishing Co., 1923), chapters 6, 7, 8, 10, 11, 12, 13.

sent. Two mixed bloods, Charles Hicks and James Vann, had played no small part behind the scenes in bringing about the favorable decision. But Doublehead took the credit. He had made his speech for a purpose. He felt that compensation was due him. When the meeting had broken up, he asked the good brothers for a bottle of whiskey.

The career of James Vann was one to wreck completely the philosophy of the dogmatic Moravian. He was a trader. With the business judgment of a Jim Bridger locating his fort on the Oregon Trail, Vann established his post in the valley of the Conasauga beside the much-traveled route to the lowlands. Within a radius of less than a score of miles rose the smokes of four important Cherokee towns: Sumac Town, Rabbit Trap, Coosawattee, and Oostanaula. Vann's Place was near the center of a nation of about fifteen thousand people.

The windows of his house looked out upon the flat fields of a broad plantation. The red soil was rich and in good years brought forth plentifully. Vann did not own the fields that stretched before his door or even the land on which his cabin stood. All the territory within the bounds of the Cherokee country was owned by the Nation. Vann, like all other members of the tribe, was only a tenant at will. But he owned his improvements, together with many cattle and Negro slaves.

According to the standards of the day Vann was rich—a privilege, according to Calvinist theory, reserved for the righteous. But unfortunately Vann, in the eyes of the gentle Moravian missionaries who established themselves at Spring Place within a few miles of his door, was a great "sinner." He enjoyed the luxury of two wives, both Cherokees. He liked nothing better at times than getting drunk. Drunk or sober, he ruled his slaves with a rod of iron. He shot one whom he caught plotting against his life; another who had robbed him he burned at the stake. By all the laws of God, as Christians understood them, such a man should not have prospered. In the end, however, Vann came fittingly to a violent end. He fell out with the husband of his sister, one John Falling. In the duel which followed Falling's bullet creased Vann's sleeve while the trader's lead made an end of his antagonist. Falling's Indian relatives invoked the ancient tribal law of retaliation. In 1809, when Vann was helping to drive a gang of thieves out of the country, the clan of Falling killed him. So passed the first benefactor of the Moravian mission to the Cherokees.

Vann's end illustrates the blend of white and Indian customs to be found in the Cherokee country in the early years of the nineteenth century. His career suggests also the position and importance of the mixed bloods. Most of these were descended from English-speaking stock, but some had a dash of French or Spanish blood. The mixed bloods were emerging as the leaders of the Nation. When the Raven Mockers swept through the Conasauga valley with many years of Vann's unlived life, the Moravian missionaries at Spring Place felt that the heavens had fallen.

When the first of them came to the Cherokee country in December, 1801, they lived at Vann's Place while their cabin was building. Since they had been forced to leave their plow behind, Vann sent to their field a half dozen teams and slaves. When the neighboring Indians grew suspicious or hostile, the trader soothed and cajoled them.

The good brothers remonstrated with their benefactor

for his Sabbath revels, but he merely laughed. When, with infinite seriousness, they brought up the subject nearest their hearts, he told them that no such person as Jesus ever lived and that the Bible was a fable. Regretfully they gave up their efforts to reconstruct their friend and protector. The missionaries had no better luck with the mixed bloods who frequented Vann's Place. The rabbit of the Cherokee myths was no more astute in escaping from his many predicaments than were these traders when they discovered the Moravian brothers stalking their souls. Turning to the many pure-blood Indians who stopped at Vann's, the indefatigable missionaries sought by gestures "to explain the love of God for them." What the redmen thought the missionaries were doing the record does not disclose.

In 1805 the first Moravians departed. At the same time Brother John Gambold and his wife, Sister Anna, looked upon the Nation to which they had dedicated their lives. At Spring Place in an environment in which every stream, every waterfall, every cave, every mountain was the abode of a Cherokee spirit or suggested a Cherokee myth the good Moravian couple sought to propagate the religion which came out of Palestine. Brother Gambold knew nothing of the friendly invisible Immortals of the mountains or of the Little Men, the wonder-working fairies of the valleys. He did not know that the redbird was the daughter of the Sun, who long ago had died of snake bite and had gone to the Darkening Land. For Brother Gambold the land of the living heathen was the Darkening Land. He gave his life to dispelling with the light of the Gospel the shadows from one small corner.

It seems never to have occurred to Gambold that the folkways of the Cherokees were the results of adjustments, running through hundreds of years, to peculiar life conditions and so were probably calculated to serve well Indian needs. If the Cherokee did not cover himself from neck to heel with clothing, it was not because he was sinful but because he got on very well without a superfluity of raiment. If the Indian dances sometimes seemed lewd, Brother Gambold forgot that he was dealing with a frank nature people who would have been puzzled and amused by the mysteries with which the early nineteenth century white American enshrouded sex. To the good brother from Salem the ways of the Cherokees were all too convincing evidence of the truth of the doctrine that all men had become depraved by Adam's fall. Gambold did not study the Cherokee culture with an eye to assisting in directing those inevitable modifications which came as a result of the changed circumstances brought about by contact with the whites. He sought to pluck out of the lives of the children entrusted to his care the folkways of the Cherokees and to substitute therefor those of Christendom and of early nineteenth century North Carolina. The measure of success which he achieved was the result of his zeal, his complete self-sacrifice, and a peculiar quality of the Cherokee mind.

The Cherokees were outstanding among the Indians for the ease and rapidity with which their culture underwent evolution. They were a forward-looking people, adaptable and eager for new things. Before the end of the eighteenth century the white frontier was pressing against their borders on the east, north, and west. They feared these whites, particularly in the years following the American Revolution. After the inauguration of Washington the kindly, paternalistic policy of the federal government quieted their apprehensions. In the War of 1812 their young men fought side by side with Andrew Jackson against the Creek Red Sticks who had taken up the tomahawk against the United States. As early as 1791 the plan of the United States was to civilize the Cherokees. In that year was written into a treaty for the purchase of land the provision that the United States annually should distribute among the Cherokees farming tools, spinning wheels, and looms. As the years passed more and more Cherokees abandoned the hunt and became planters and cattle men. Necessity played a part in the change. The advance of the white frontier restricted the range of the Cherokee hunter and the insatiable demand of London for furs depleted the game. The mixed blood, Charles Hicks, who during much of the second decade of the nineteenth century was the leader behind the scenes of the tribal government, worked unceasingly to persuade his people to accept the ways of the white man. On Good Friday in 1813 Hicks, before a congregation of Indians and mixed bloods which filled the rude barn at Spring Place, knelt at the feet of Brother Gambold and was baptized. The moment was charged with emotion. Mingled with the missionary's solemn words was the sobbing of Hicks' full-blood Cherokee wife and of the children of the Spring Place school.

The Cherokees had ceased to suspect the humble Moravian brethren. Brother Gambold was a farmer, carpenter, and general mechanic. Aided by the boys of the school and by one or two Moravian helpers, he housed and fed the little group of adults and pupils which made up the mission. Never did he refuse provisions and shelter to Indians who passed the door. There were nights when his living room was so full of sleeping redmen that he and his wife had scarcely a place to lay their heads. There were times also when generosity forced the mission to face hunger. But always supplies came in. For sixteen years he labored without a furlough. He received a little financial assistance from the brethren in North Carolina and, for a time, a paltry hundred dollars a year from the government. He did not seek many converts, but he changed for all time the lives of those he won. Though his mental outlook was narrow and his solution for the puzzling problem of the Indians contained many flaws, his life of unselfishness enabled him to help them to better things. But Sister Anna, rather than her husband, was the soul of the mission.

Before she went to Spring Place she had been a teacher in one of the Moravian schools for girls. In Georgia she gave herself unreservedly to the Indian and mixed blood children who lived in the school. She helped to make their clothes and supervised the Negro slave who cooked their meals. She nursed them when they were sick and taught them reading, writing, and arithmetic when they were well. She saw to their religious education and instructed them in weaving and spinning. A botanic garden in which grew many exotic plants, including some medicinal herbs, was the result of her management. She took her scholars on rambles through the fields and in the mountains. A prominent English Moravian scholar and naturalist from England visited Spring Place on an American tour. "On my expressing a wish to see some of the botanical products of that country," he commented later, "Sister Gambold sent me, last autumn, between twelve and fourteen hundred specimens of dried plants, besides near a hundred packages of seeds, several minerals, specimens of all the Indian manufacture of cane, etc., and a number of other curiosities, apologizing for not having done more as the season was unfavourable; whereas I should have thought the collecting of these a good half year's work for one person's undivided attention, under the most favourable circumstances. And yet this person, banished as she is from civilized society, cheerfully laboring year after year with scarcely any promise of success, yet undauntedly persevering, was the first teacher in the Bethlehem Young Ladies' Seminary, and seemed its main support.... To any not devoted to the cause of God ... the sacrifice might appear almost too great...." Whatever one may think of the theology of the Spring Place missionaries, theirs was a living religion.

One of the brightest of Sister Gambold's pupils was Galagina, "The Buck." During the years of his adolescence she trained his mind and moulded his character. His later important career in the Cherokee Nation was built on the foundations which she laid. In 1818 when he was about fifteen years old she sent him off to the mission school founded the year before at Cornwall, Connecticut. After he had shaken off his homesickness, The Buck, who in traveling north had taken the name of his benefactor, Elias Boudinot, wrote to his former teachers, loading his paragraphs with the phrases he had learned at Spring Place.

"Dear Friends, It was with grief and sorrow the last letter I wrote you. I said that my sorrow was more than I could bare.... Pray for me that my faith fail not, and that I may be useful to my countrymen and also pray for my countrymen who are in this school.... Methink I hear the Saviour say, 'Son, go and work today in my vineyard.' Lord, I obey, here am I, send me among the heathen.

"This letter need correcting but as it is vacation and our instructor is not well, I will send it as it is. Elias Boudinot."

PART II
THE LITCHFIELD HILLS

4

Obookiah

IT is not known how the young Indian, Elias Boudinot, came to Cornwall in the northwest corner of Connecticut. He may have journeyed overland by horseback and stagecoach all the way from his southern mountains. If he came by water, he must have seen some of the ports and thriving river towns of the state. Connecticut was stirring with new life in the first quarter of the nineteenth century. Some men were adventuring in sailing ships to ever more distant seas and ports in pursuit of trade. Others were throwing dams across the smaller streams and were using the impounded water to turn water wheels. Crude, clattering factories were appearing in the valley bottoms. Perhaps Boudinot passed some of these on his way to Cornwall in the Litchfield Hills. These hills, perhaps, reminded him of home.

They are well worn, these resistant cores of peaks that in a distant geologic past towered above the snow line. Here and there deep scratches in the quartz and feldspar recall the time when the continental ice sheet covered them. The ice cap left behind a debris of erratic boulders scattered through the hills as a careless husbandman might cast his seed. When Boudinot came, farmers were still each spring picking a new crop of stones off their fields to dispose of in great piles or to use in building stone wall fences.

The hills, covered with vegetation to their summits, are high enough to achieve dignity; but they are not majestic as are the mountains whence the Indian came. On the western side of these uplands Boudinot found Cornwall, a tiny agricultural village. Above its cluster of farmhouses rose Colt's Foot Mountain.

Faithful to New England tradition the houses of Cornwall were built around a green. Beside this common stood a small building which housed the Foreign Mission School. The institution was scarcely more than a year old when the young Cherokee first enrolled. But its fame had already spread far enough to bring young Boudinot from a Moravian mission in the southern Appalachians.

The Foreign Mission School was evidence of the power of Protestant Christianity over the people of Connecticut. Even as a new industrial age was rising, a dream, incredibly bold, was taking form in the minds of the Puritans who lived beside the Housatonic, the Farmington, and the Thames. For them the function of religion was not merely to conserve ancient values. Their faith was a dynamic force whose destiny was to transform the world. It caused the simple husbandman whose horizon lay only a short distance beyond his acres to vision empires to be conquered by Truth. The Foreign Mission School was the concrete embodiment of that dream.

As the boy, Elias Boudinot, adjusted himself to his new surroundings, he heard from time to time snatches of the strange story that lay behind the founding of the school. He listened to accounts of another boy, a Polynesian only a little older than himself, whose name was Obookiah and who had come from that distant region known as the

Hawaiian Islands. Perhaps young Boudinot in his walks about Cornwall passed in the cemetery Obookiah's grave marked with an impressive headstone. The story was a compound of tragedy and triumph.[1]

Obookiah, it seems, had been a victim of bloody tribal wars that swept his island home in the first decade of the nineteenth century. Massacre had orphaned him while he was still little more than a child. One of the chiefs of the victorious party had adopted the boy with the design, no doubt, of rearing him to be a warrior. When, however, Obookiah saw his captors fling his father's sister over a cliff, he fled. Ultimately he found refuge and respite from war in the hut of an uncle, an old shaman who made sacrifices to wooden idols grimacing at one another across a temple enclosure. Obookiah with a sinking heart discovered that he had escaped the terrors of battle only to find himself surrounded by the supernatural horrors of restless ghosts and malignant deities.

Again the boy ran away. About the year 1807 he fled his homeland as cabin boy for a certain Captain Brintnall whose sturdy square-rigger hailed from New Haven, Connecticut. Brintnall was venturing in the China trade. After the captain returned to America about 1809, Henry Obookiah—for that is what the skipper called him—was left in New Haven like a bit of flotsam washed up on the beach by the tide. He became the first Polynesian explorer of Connecticut who has left an account of his experiences with the natives.

Elias Boudinot, homesick for Spring Place and his southern mountains, could sympathize with the stranded Poly-

[1] This chapter is based on Edwin Welles Dwight, *Memoirs of Henry Obookiah* ... (Elizabethtown, N. J., Edson Hart, publisher, 1819).

nesian boy. As the Indian listened to the story from the lips of the principal of the school and, perhaps, from those of Timothy Stone, the Cornwall minister, he must have been drawn to this dark-skinned wanderer whom he had never seen. Boudinot was wise enough to sense that, had it not been for Obookiah, Galagina would never have had an opportunity for an education in the North.

※

Henry Obookiah, still the servant of the kindly Brintnall in New Haven, wandered vaguely through the streets of what had been before the Embargo a busy little seaport of some six thousand inhabitants. Had he known more English he would have heard idlers about the wharves raging at those two malevolent Virginians, Jefferson and Madison. Tempers cooled a little, about the time of Brintnall's return, when New Haven learned that a Non-Intercourse Act had been substituted for the hated Embargo. Barrels and bales were rolled out of warehouses and there was much scrubbing of ships' decks. Henry, clad in his sailor's garb, did not fail to notice the impressive wigs, the short clothes, the silk stockings, and the buckled shoes of the great merchants who daily came down to their offices near the waterfront.

He gradually sensed that the row of plain brick buildings in the yard beside the central green was inhabited by young men not far from his own age who were being taught by masters. One day, as he loitered near these buildings of Yale College, a curious undergraduate paused to talk to him. In broken English Obookiah informed the stranger that he would like to learn the white man's language and ways. The next day Henry's formal education began in the room of "Mr. E.W.D."

Obookiah was delighted. He was finding the Connecticut Yankees an unexpectedly friendly people. He tried hard to learn. "Mr. D" was so much impressed that in a short time he suggested that his protégé leave the house of the good captain to reside in that of the Reverend Timothy Dwight, president of the college. At the moment President Dwight was triumphant in his great battle against indifference and infidelity. For years he had been smiting hip and thigh the materialism of Hobbes and the popular deism of Tom Paine. Had Obookiah's eyes been rightly trained, he could have seen, even as he crossed it, a dejected Lucifer slinking off into a far corner of the college campus. Knowledge of the Hawaiian had come to the president and he was anxious to inspect at first hand this representative of heathendom where the Evil One was still supreme. So Obookiah became a member of the household of the man who was, at the moment, the greatest figure in New England. "This satisfied me," wrote the naïve Henry. "I lived with this pious and good family for some time." To pass in about two years from the hut of a Hawaiian shaman to the house of the high priest of American Puritanism was Obookiah's strange fate. At a later time Connecticut people saw in the episode a convincing illustration of the hand of God shaping the destinies of men.

Obookiah's quick mind and winning manners seem to have impressed "Pope" Dwight that here was a brand worth rescuing from the burning. The president decided he should have an opportunity to learn and turned him over to a Litchfield County minister, for Connecticut education was still to a considerable extent in the hands of the clergy. Henry found himself in a quiet little village on the banks of the Naugatuck River far in the interior of the state, where he lived and studied in the house of the Reverend Mr. Mills, the pastor of Torringford (Torrington). Here he had regular lessons in speaking, reading and writing English. As the hard-working Henry slowly penetrated the mysteries of the strange culture he found in Connecticut and began to see his new friends as they saw themselves, he discovered, to his dismay, that for a second time he had fallen into the hands of a shaman. It was true that the grave Mr. Mills did not indulge in wild chants before wooden images, but he said long prayers to what seemed to be nothing at all. He did not affect a flamboyant regalia on ceremonial occasions, but his garb set him off from the rest of the people. Finally and conclusively, Mr. Mills, like the abandoned uncle, made dealing with the supernatural his chief business in life. To make matters worse he was not the only shaman to come within the Hawaiian boy's horizon. Connecticut ministers flocked to Torringford to see heathendom in the flesh. For a time Connecticut seemed to the unhappy Obookiah a country peopled almost entirely with clergymen. "I was known by a great number of Ministers," he commented glumly. "But on account of my ignorance of the true God, I do not wish to hear them when they talk to me. I would not wish to be in the room where they were; neither did I wish to come near to a Minister, for the reason that he should talk to me about God, whom I hated to hear. I was told by them about Heaven and Hell, but I did not pay any attention to what they say; for I thought I was just as happy as the other people, as those who do know about God much more than I do."

Obookiah passed from the home of Mr. Mills to that newly established hot house of evangelical Puritanism,

Andover Theological Seminary, where he offered the students an opportunity to practice on a heathen. He became the center of interest in a sort of missionary clinic. Once, in vacation time, he escaped for a brief space from the surveillance of the clergy and, tasting a mild freedom, learned that there was gaiety as well as soberness among Connecticut people. But the discovery came too late. That supernatural world which the pious Mr. Mills had pictured again and again to his recalcitrant pupil encompassed him, closed in on him, and claimed him for its own. As Obookiah, laboring for a farmer, worked alone in the woods one day, a haunting fear crept into his heart. Beneath the superficial loveliness of the Connecticut hills he seemed to see a seething lake of fire, as though the lava-spattered crater of his own Kilauea were yawning at his feet. "I thought that if I should then die, I must certainly be cast off forever. While I was working it appeared as if it was a voice saying, 'Cut it down, why cumbereth it the ground,' ... I worked no longer—but dropped my axe. I fell upon my knees and looked up to the Almighty Jehovah for help. I was but an undone and hell-deserving sinner." Obookiah had managed to escape the Hawaiian shaman; but the magic of Mr. Mills succeeded. How jealous the old uncle would have been, as he laid his hog on the sacrificial altar, if he could have known the terrors which his profession in Connecticut could conjure up!

※

Several years passed. Obookiah became fairly proficient in English. He even made an attempt to translate the Bible into his native tongue. He became a professing Christian and the fear of Hell was replaced by the comforting assurance of salvation. He wished to return to his own country as a teacher and missionary of his new faith. Then to the Puritan Yankee Obookiah became a symbol, personifying heathendom, once dying in darkness, brought to new life by the light of the Gospel. When he spoke in churches, this son of Polynesia warmed the hearts and roused the imaginations of the undemonstrative Puritans. Under the guidance of a clerical tutor, the same E.W.D. who had helped him at Yale, he wrote in 1816 an account of his life, and the narrative became a popular tract.

The progress of Obookiah toward grace called attention to other South Sea islanders whom the sea had cast up on the shores of New England. The Puritans, encouraged, planned a school where all the other dusky strangers could prepare themselves to carry the light of the true faith to their own peoples. After much consultation they decided to locate the new institution in the tiny village of Cornwall in the midst of the Litchfield hills. Obookiah traveled among the churches. He called the people of Connecticut to come over into Macedonia. With the Hawaiian boy as a symbol of the opportunities for conquering heathendom, the clergy succeeded in their campaign for funds. The bold venture of founding a mission school resulted in triumph.

Tragedy, however, trod hard on the heels of missionary success. In late December, 1817, when the school which in a sense had been founded for him had not yet completed its first year, Henry Obookiah took to his bed with typhus fever. Timothy Stone without hesitation removed the sick boy from the dormitory of the school to his own home. There Mary Stone forgot for a time her familiar household worries as she gave herself up to the task of fighting the dangerous fever. She became both nurse and mother to this orphaned son of Polynesia with whom life had dealt so strangely. Cornwall winters are cold and the woman, busying herself at the bedside, paused often to put another log on the fire. She read to her patient at length from the Bible. He grew better, then worse. The doctor became uncertain; there were consultations of physicians. At last hope was abandoned, "As death seemed to approach Mrs. S. said to him, 'Henry, do you think you are dying?' He answered, 'Yes, ma'am'—and often said, 'Mrs. S. I thank you for your kindness.' She said, 'I wish we might meet hereafter.' He replied, 'I hope we shall'—and taking her hand, affectionately bid her farewell."[2] A few days later Lyman Beecher rode over from Litchfield through the cold to preach the sermon over the coffin of Obookiah.

Within the preceding year the mantle of Timothy Dwight had fallen on the shoulders of Beecher. When the great Yale president passed away in 1817, the Litchfield pastor became the leader of the Connecticut clergy. One of the founders of the Mission School and a member of its Board of Agents, he discovered himself, as he followed the highway through Goshen, confronting a difficult task. In the midst of the school's first year the Almighty had cut off none other than Obookiah, that symbol of heathendom saved from darkness who had made the Mission School possible. Would the literal-minded interpret the Hawaiian's death as evidence of the Lord's disapproval of the Cornwall enterprise? Lyman Beecher was determined that this outpost on the frontier of the Kingdom should continue.

Addressing the faithful who, clad in their Sunday best,

[2] *Ibid.*, 103 f.

sat in solemn silence near the departed, Lyman Beecher used to the full that skill for which he was famous beyond the bounds of Connecticut. He conjured up a vision which contained an argument. "Nor do we feel as if our labor had been lost, did our work terminate this day. If any are disposed to think so, let them behold the dying scene of Henry Obookiah; witness his heavenly smile; trace his bright path to glory; behold his immaculate spirit before the throne of God—his astonishment at the Providence which brought him from Owhyhee, to fit him for Heaven, and his rapture at the glory revealed in him. Behold his humility, while he veils his face, and casts his crown at the feet of Jesus; his rapture while he cries amid the myriads of glory, 'Worthy is the Lamb that was slain' ... Who would dare to stop the song which he sings, to extinguish the rapture which he feels, to eclipse by his removal from Heaven the glory of God, which his redemption illustrates, or rob angels of their joy at his conversion, and their augmented joy at his arrival in glory."[3]

As an inspiration for the men of New England to go forth to war upon the idols of heathendom, Obookiah dead was more powerful than Obookiah living. The school went on. Six months after the passing of the Hawaiian, Elias Boudinot, Cherokee, joined the company of students who lived and worked beside Cornwall green.

[3] *Ibid.*, Appendix, "A Sermon . . . by Lyman Beecher," 29 f.

5

Benjamin Gold

NOT far from the Cornwall green stood the home of Benjamin Gold, leading man in the community, an agent of the Foreign Mission School, and a person destined to play an important role in the life of Elias Boudinot. Gold knew Obookiah. For Benjamin Gold the fall of 1817 was unusually somber, because in December the Hawaiian boy lay at the point of death. The Litchfield hills, their autumn splendor gone, waited the coming of winter. The flaming colors that decked their slopes a few weeks before had faded to brownish gray, splotched here and there with the dark green of pines and hemlocks, the whole merging in the distance into a blue haze. In Cornwall the flower beds beside the houses displayed only the withered stalks of frost-killed hollyhocks and chrysanthemums.

But these dead stalks did not symbolize Agent Benjamin Gold's hopes for the school. Cornwall people were accustomed to adversity. Each recurring winter was a season of hardship and death. Harriet, Benjamin's youngest daughter, once wrote of a January in the Litchfield hills. "It is quite sickly in C. and deaths are frequent—Widow Joseph Judson died last week after a fourteen days illness—the fever which she died with and which so many are sick with is the same as prevailed and swept off so many several years ago—The bell has just been tolling for Mr. Shepherd's son, about 20 years of age—Widow David Patterson is almost gone with consumption." The slow rhythm of the church bell spoke of nature's ultimate victory over the individual.

The men and women of Cornwall sought to adjust their lives not only to the peculiarities of the Litchfield hills but to a world of the imagination encompassed by the Christian theology which had dominated the thought of the Middle Ages. Dante, Milton, and Michael Angelo were but a few of the creators of its landscapes and inhabitants. The eighteenth century had seen the rise of new ideas which jarred with older Christian concepts; the Age of Enlightenment had sniffed at devils and angels. But in the Litchfield hills, as in Connecticut generally, Milton's God yet reigned. Timothy Stone preached in the church beside Cornwall green in a day when a strong race was moving swiftly westward to the conquest of a continent and when along the banks of the very streams about him the foundations of a new industrial era were being laid. Yet he, and his fellow Puritans, put emphasis on the inner life. The years of a man were not so much an opportunity for living as a preparation for a life to come. Benjamin Gold built his life on what he believed to be eternal Truth.

A road, ancestor to the modern concrete thoroughfare, climbed from Cornwall, sheltered by a ring of hills, to Goshen on a wind-swept plateau. It was an artery along which flowed the life of rural Connecticut. Benjamin Gold knew every house beside this highway.[1] He had traveled it as a child in the days before the Revolution. It had been his

---

[1] For brief biographies of some members of the Gold family, see Edward C. Starr, *A History of Cornwall, Connecticut, a Typical New England Town* (New Haven, Conn., Tuttle, Morehouse & Taylor Co., 1926), 305-08, and T. S. Gold, *Historical Records of the Town of Cornwall, Litchfield County, Connecticut* (Hartford, Case, Lockwood & Brainerd Co., 1877), 289-94, 411-22.

path on countless business trips to Litchfield. Since 1802 he had regularly climbed the hill to Goshen as he started on his journey to Hartford or New Haven to attend, as representative of Cornwall, the successive sessions of the General Assembly. The road brought customers from the northern part of the town to his store under the shadow of Colt's Foot Mountain.

Fifty-seven years had hardened the character and strengthened the self-reliance of this Connecticut Puritan. Like his Cornwall neighbors he was a husbandman. His farm lay in level fields not far from the village green in bottom lands that the local people called the "plains." He himself had built the house which sat a little back from the highway, a plain but dignified dwelling, displaying the beauty of Georgian line and proportion. It was a fitting habitation for the son of a Bachelor of Arts who was himself a man of consequence in the Litchfield hills. The barns stood in the rear.

As deacon of the Cornwall church Benjamin Gold had supported the establishment of the Foreign Mission School at Cornwall and had contributed handsomely to the institution. He took a solid satisfaction in its opening in May, 1817. That year was one of the happiest in his life. He must have felt he was carrying forward his father's work.

Hezekiah Gold, Benjamin's father, had preached in the First Church of Cornwall for the greater part of his life. This Revolutionary divine was a strange man who, after graduating from Yale College, made his home in the Litchfield hills. Many times Benjamin had read the laudatory inscription on his father's tombstone and had contrasted it with the whispers of enemies that the dead man had been a lifeless preacher and that he had devoted too much of his energy to the acquiring and managing of one of the finest farms in the town. Whatever might be the truth of these charges, one fact was clear — the elder Gold had independence of character. He had been a Patriot in Revolutionary days. In those times, when excitement ran high and tempers were short, confronting a schism in his church, he had set his face against a majority of his parishioners and had stood fast. He accumulated enough substance to send two sons to Yale. Benjamin did not go to college but, in his turn, sent two sons to the college in New Haven.

One of these, Ruggles Gold, was even more influential than Benjamin in bringing the Foreign Mission School to Cornwall.[2] Ruggles represented a rare type of early nineteenth century Puritanism, He had been a sickly farm boy, much given to books. As a youth it was hard for him to hold the plow handles behind the oxen or to stow away hay in mows filled to the square-hewn plates. Benjamin Gold sent him to college when he was fifteen, and he became a member of the class of 1806. At Yale the adolescent boy sat at the feet of Timothy Dwight, brilliant, kindly, overwhelming. As a sculptor moulds the clay to his will, Dwight shaped the character of his students. His touch was sure, for he had no doubts regarding the nature and pattern of the good life. His methods were personal evangelism and reasoned preaching. Many times, after a sermon of his in the college chapel, he saw the boys who roomed in the Old Brick Row come, filled with inspiration, to the altar. Dwight sent Ruggles back to Cornwall a dynamo of spiritual energy housed in a fragile body. After the founding of

[2] For Ruggles Gold see also Franklin B. Dexter, *Biographical Sketches of the Graduates of Yale College with Annals of the College History*, VI (New Haven, Yale University Press, 1912), 31.

the school, however, his work was done. Declining health kept him inactive.

If Ruggles Gold typified the dynamic faith of Puritanism, Timothy Stone, who stood in the pulpit of Hezekiah Gold, personified some other characteristics of the organized Congregational Church.[3] Pastor Stone was a man of mediocre mind who had attended Yale but did not graduate. In 1803 he became minister of the Cornwall church at an annual stipend of four hundred and twenty-four dollars, a salary that was not sufficient to enable him to give his two sons the educational opportunities which he had enjoyed. He was a poor man in a dignified office. It fell to the lot of Mary Stone, his wife, to enforce that pinching economy which kept her less careful husband out of debt. At the same time she had to stretch an inadequate income to maintain a standard of living commensurate with a clergyman's position in life. Mary Stone's survival for four score years suggests the stamina of Connecticut stock.

Timothy was imposing in body if not in mind. Like the organized church, which he represented, he sought to maintain an outward grandeur which sometimes concealed a lack of power within. When he strode across the village green, he insisted that young men and boys remove their hats at a considerable distance before meeting him. On Sundays, however, though he preached dull sermons on the time-honored tenets of Puritanism, he was, for the moment, the central figure in the community. Going to meeting was still one of the most potent of Connecticut folkways. The people, moreover, recognized that Timothy Stone, with all his narrowness and absurdities, was fundamentally sincere.

[3] For a biography of Stone, see Starr, *A History of Cornwall*, 375 f. There is much autobiographical material in Stone's "Historical Sketches of the Churches of Cornwall, Conn.," in Gold, *Historical Records*, 42-94.

He visited faithfully the sick and the bereaved. He was a veritable watchdog over the morals of the community. He boasted that for twenty years before he left the church in 1827 "there was scarcely an instance of a midnight dance or party of the youth known in ... Cornwall."[4] In 1817 the Reverend Timothy at the age of forty-three reached the climax of his life with the opening of the Foreign Mission School. He had persuaded his flock to provide the small two-story building on the green where the scholars roomed and recited. He was himself one of the Board of Agents. Most important of all, Obookiah, famous throughout New England, was now a student in Cornwall and a member of his congregation.

[4] Gold, *Historical Records*, 71.

6

The Foreign Mission School

SUNDAY, May 6, 1818, saw an unwonted stir in Cornwall. The Reverend Joseph Harvey, A.M., pastor of the church in Goshen, was in town, and what was more important, John Treadwell, former governor of Connecticut and a leader in missionary activities, had driven over in his carriage. The unusual Sabbath bustle centered in the small two-story, gambrel-roofed building in which were the classrooms of the Foreign Mission School, polished for inspection. A cosmopolitan handful of scholars prepared for the exciting event of inaugurating a principal. The three classrooms in the schoolhouse, an improvised dormitory, and the principal's home comprised the meager equipment with which was established at Cornwall a base of operations for a proposed advance against the frontier of the Kingdom of Darkness.

The Mission School was evidence that the horizon of the people of Cornwall was not limited to the hills which they could see from their doorsteps. The institution was the product of that same restless, imaginative American mind which expresses itself in the twentieth century in gigantic industrial enterprises and world-wide commercial conquests.

Doubtless many of the Gold family were in the audience which assembled on May 6 in Timothy Stone's church to witness the inauguration of the Reverend Herman Daggett. The occasion was a solemn one. The mysticism which Jonathan Edwards had contributed to Puritanism filled the hushed congregation with the sense of the immanent presence of God. Surely He was present where a unique outpost of the Kingdom was being established. Treadwell rose impressively. "The great object of the Foreign Mission School," he said, "is, to afford a hospitable asylum for such unevangelized youth, of good promise, as are, or shall be, providentially brought to our shores, and cast upon us; or, as shall be found within our limits; and to furnish them with such instruction in the English tongue, as shall qualify them to read and understand the Sacred Scriptures in that language . . . also in the elements of general science—in the principles and practice of modern agriculture—in the more common and useful arts of civilized life—and when circumstances shall lead the way, and shew their utility, in physic and surgery—also in the learned languages, such especially, as bid fair to become preachers of the Gospel, or translators of the Sacred Volume."

Turning, the governor addressed Daggett: "I do, therefore, in the name and behalf of the agents of this institution, by the delivery of these keys to your care and keeping, which you will view as the symbol of office, thus publicly induct you into the office of Principal of the Foreign Mission School here established. . . . Make it your great, your only object, to train the youth committed to your charge, for distinguished service among their countrymen in some department of missionary service."[1]

Herman Daggett,[2] the frail man of fifty-two to whom the

---

[1] The address is printed as an appendix to Dwight, *Memoirs of Henry Obookiah*.

[2] For a biography of Daggett, see Starr, *A History of Cornwall*, 291.

ex-governor handed the badge of office, must have seemed a feeble warrior to invade the lair of the Prince of Evil. Since graduating with honors from Brown he had alternated between preaching and combating ill health. Lyman Beecher, an agent of the school, had discovered Daggett and had shrewdly judged his man. Besides a trained intellect and a kindly disposition, the new principal had courage. It required courage for a man to engage himself for five hundred dollars a year to instruct and discipline, with little aid, the sons of the uncivilized tribes of the world.

Polynesians, Melanesians, Chinese, and American Indians from several nations, together with American boys training for the mission field took their seats in the schoolroom overlooking the Cornwall green. The earnest Daggett would have been wounded had one compared to the Tower of Babel the school exercise in which the pupils addressed the audience, each in his native tongue. The dormitory where the scholars bunked was a potpourri of races, the setting for an adventure in the brotherhood of man. The Foreign Mission School was the product of Puritanism galvanized by a new missionary zeal.

Three years passed. The school flourished, conclusive evidence to the Puritan mind of divine approbation. The work of managing the institution became so heavy that Herman Vaill, a young candidate for the ministry, was retained to assist the principal. Vaill divided his attentions between the heathen and Flora Gold, daughter of Benjamin. Flora was persuaded, but the judgment of Cornwall regarding the assistant seems to have been divided. The American propensity to inscribe sentiments in public places transformed the back of a gallery pew in Timothy Stone's church into a historical document.

> *The eloquence of Herman Vaill*
> *Would make the stoutest sinner quail.*

wrote an admirer to which couplet another added:

> *The hissing goose has far more sense*
> *Than Vaill with all his eloquence.*[3]

The efforts of Vaill and Daggett prospered. Both pupils and support increased. In New England the new enthusiasm for foreign missions was at flood tide. Obookiah, known to an ever widening circle through his *Memoirs,* had become a Puritan saint and, thanks to Beecher's sermon, his death had become an apotheosis. Periodically in the *Religious Intelligencer* and in the current newspapers the conscientious Timothy Stone, agent in charge of donations, recorded the gifts which came to the school. "The Female Cent Society" of Sharon, Connecticut, forwarded some fulled cloth, socks, mittens, and a skein of yarn. "The Female Charitable Society" of Winsted sent suspenders, drawers, and a pair of pantaloons. Native garb was deemed inappropriate for the Kingdom. Other contributing organizations in the Reverend Timothy's list were "The Female Dorcas Society" of North Hartford, "The Female Charitable Praying Society" of Westford, and "The Female Fragment Society" of Salisbury. But the ladies were not the only givers. A Goshen farmer planted a missionary field which yielded thirty-five bushels of corn.

[3] *Ibid.,* 382.

A deacon from North Cornwall gave two barrels of cider. The fame of the school spread beyond the bounds of New England. A man in Rochester on the New York frontier sent two hundred dollars. Elias Boudinot of New Jersey, one of the greatest philanthropists of the day, left a legacy of five hundred dollars to the institution in which was enrolled the Cherokee boy who had taken his name. In 1820 Baron de Campagne, of Basel sent from Switzerland one hundred ducats.

The Baron requested that letters especially written by students of the school be sent him. Principal Daggett chose his brightest pupils, two Cherokees, David Brown and Elias Boudinot. In his reply to these messages Campagne enclosed fifteen hundred florins.

Boudinot's letter presents a sample of the ideas which Daggett and Vaill thought the heathen needed. Half hidden by the pious phrases of the current Puritan jargon can be glimpsed, however, the mind of an Indian boy who was one day to achieve a place in the history of his people. Perhaps Harriet Gold in her late teens read the letter in the *Religious Intelligencer* where the principal, in obedience to sound canons of publicity, had it published.

"Honoured and respected Sir—Having been requested by my beloved teacher, Mr. Daggett, I have the pleasure of writing to you; and, in the name of my fellow students, to thank you for your benevolent donation of 100 ducats. We feel thankful to the Giver of every good and perfect gift, that we are not destitute of Christian friends who are willing to give their property for our sustenance, while receiving an education in this charitable institution. We are here far from our native countries, brought here by the kind providence of God; and blessed be his name, that he has given us friends to support us, and to instruct us in human knowledge, but especially in that science which treats about the immortal soul, and the only everlasting felicity. ... I am a Cherokee, from a nation of Indians living in the southern part of the United States. There are eight of us here from that nation. Six out of eight profess to be followers of the meek and lowly Jesus. I came to this school more than two years ago; and, if it be the will of God, I expect to leave it in about one or two years. I feel sometimes an ardent desire to return to my countrymen and to teach them the way of salvation. Pray for me that my faith fail not, and that I may not finally prove insincere. That we may meet in the kingdom, which is eternal in the heavens, is the wish of your unworthy and unknown young friend, Elias Boudinot."[4]

In the March following Elias Boudinot's letter to the benevolent baron, the Foreign Mission School and the family of Benjamin Gold experienced a sensation. A distinguished traveler from the British Isles visited Cornwall and lodged with the Golds. Adam Hodgson, Esquire, partner in an important Liverpool commercial enterprise, on a trip through the United States in 1821, did not turn aside to visit Cornwall out of chance curiosity. In England he had already heard much of the Mission School and had a lively sympathy with its aims. Perhaps in a copy of Hodgson's *Letters,* which Samuel Whiting of New York published in 1823, Herman Daggett and the Gold family read what their guest of a day had to say of them. "The country became dreary and uninteresting as we approached Goshen; but on drawing near to Cornwall, about sunset,

[4] *Religious Intelligencer,* IV, 166 f.

The Foreign Mission School at Cornwall, Connecticut

we had some beautiful mountain scenery. ... As we descended into the little valley in which the Mission School is situated, the distant mountains were fading from our view; but we had just daylight enough to see the steeple of the church, and the very few houses which seemed to compose this little village. ... The snow contributed to prolong our twilight. ... Being informed that a certain Mr.—[Benjamin Gold],[5] though not keeping a regular inn, sometimes received those who visited the school, I applied to him, in preference to taking up my quarters in a very uninviting tavern. I soon obtained admittance into a neat little chamber, where I sat up till a late hour, indulging the very interesting reflections naturally excited by my situation, in a deep retired romantic valley, where so many heathen youths were collected from different parts of the world, to be instructed in the principles of the Christian religion.

"I rose early, and at six o'clock, when the bell rang, went to the school of prayers. A chapter in the New Testament was first read, each pupil, or rather several of them, taking a verse in succession; afterwards, David Brown, alias Awik, a half-breed Cherokee ... led the devotions of the assembly; they then all dispersed to their own rooms. ... I have obtained a list of the native names of the scholars for you; but in the mean time, must tell you, that there were, among others, one Malay, one Otaheitan, two Mowhees, two Owhyhees, one New Zealander, eight Cherokee Indians, two Choctaws, three Muh-he-con-nuks, one Eneida, one Tuscarora, and two Coughnewagas. Three of them, Awik, David Brown a Cherokee, Kub-le-ga-nah Elias Boudinot a Cherokee, and Irepoah, an Owhyhee, afterwards

---

[5] Starr, *A History of Cornwall*, 142.

paid me a visit in my room, and sat with me half an hour. They could all speak English. ... The principal of the school said that Kub-le-ga-nah had gone through a course of history, geography, and surveying, had read some books of Virgil, and was then engaged in studying Enfield's philosophy, over which, indeed, I afterwards found him, when I visited the school. I also saw his trigonometrical copybooks. ...

"My hostess was the grand-daughter of the former pastor of the village; and the family seemed much interested with Mr. Legh Richmond's 'Little Jane,' which I left with them [a best-seller of the day dealing with village life in the Isle of Wight]. It was a great pleasure to me to read it in this little valley, with all the associations with which it seemed so well to harmonize. We left Cornwall at ten o'clock, on the 3d, in an open sleigh. Our road, for three or four miles, lay through a natural grove of hemlock spruce, ... and cedar, which hung over our path, and whose matted boughs and dark green leaves, formed a fine contrast with the new fallen snow, which rested upon them in masses, or fell through and gave a softer appearance to the frozen surface over which we traveled."[6]

Within three years after Adam Hodgson bade farewell to it the "deep retired romantic valley" which he so much admired became the stage for a bitter drama of race prejudice and passion.

[6] Adam Hodgson, *Letters from North America* ... (London, Hurst, Robinson & Co., 1824), II, 288-300.

7

Isaiah Bunce

IN April, 1824, Isaiah Bunce, editor of *The American Eagle,* sat at his desk in Litchfield with a letter before him. It had been posted at Cornwall and bore the signatures of eight substantial men of that village. The name of Benjamin Gold topped the list. Bunce read the communication with close attention partly because it contained a shrewd thrust at him. When he had finished, he folded the epistle and returned it to Cornwall informing its authors that he would not publish it.

Bunce was an independent Yankee with a sharp wit who found newspaper editing a congenial business. Through the small rectangular panes of the window which lighted his sanctum he viewed with an eye to profits the Litchfield scene. "Thursday night last," narrated the *Eagle,* "a fellow calling himself Michael Bloomer, alledging that he had been taken by pirates, and within a few days past had been employed as an hostler at one of the inns of this place, was committed to jail, on a charge of stealing a horse from the inn at which he was employed, on the evening before. On Thursday it was discovered that the horse and hostler were missing, also that a barber's shop and dwelling had been broken open and a gold watch, pocket pistol, and 30 or 40 dollars in money taken from a trunk therein. The barber pursued toward the north, and found that the hostler, with his horse had tarried all night at an inn in Goshen, only six miles from this, and had started at sunrise, and proceeded on to the north. Before noon the barber found that rum and the devil (for Indians lay everything to the former and whitefolks to the latter) had got him neck and heels across the highway, ready to surrender him into the hands of the barber, who obtained his horse, his watch, his pistol, and some of the money, and surrendered him to our officers, by whom he was committed to prison for trial."[1]

The unhappy affair of Michael Bloomer suggests some characteristics of the life which the editor observed in the Litchfield hills. Man dealt personally with man. The barber ran down his thief and turned him over to the officers of the law. There were no impersonal and powerful organizations, such as the twentieth century knows so well, to confuse the pattern of the social fabric. Life lay open to all. A man had difficulty in hiding his character or his affairs from his neighbors. The people were governed by a simple code of morals, sanctioned by a theology the main points of which could be easily understood. Individualism was of the essence of Connecticut folkways.

The editor of the *Eagle* was a conservative in a day of change. The frontier was a lodestone drawing husbandmen away from the Connecticut hills. Stone wall fences which once had separated fields of grain were being swallowed up by outward creeping woodlots. The first clatter of industrialism was attracting Yankees from their old villages on the hilltops to the dams at the valley bottoms. Bunce regretted the influence of the frontier, but he favored

[1] *Eagle*, January 20, 1823.

industrial change. Paradoxically he mourned the passing of the age of homespun. Homespun for him symbolized industry and thrift. The Litchfield editor watched with apprehension the corrosion of the characters of his aristocratic neighbors by a growing love for luxury.

There were other changes in Connecticut, however, even more alarming. The old religion upon which rested the very foundations of society had fallen upon critical days. In 1818 the political power in the state of the Congregational clergy had been broken when Connecticut had replaced its colonial charter with a constitution. But defeat did not weaken the churches. Revivals which had begun many years before the political crisis assisted Puritanism to maintain its ancient strength. In spite of Congregational efforts to maintain preëminence, however, new sects were waxing in strength.

"Free thinking," the progeny of eighteenth century deism, was passing from community to community by underground channels and now and again was appearing in broad daylight. Bunce took an occasional fling at the new sects, and he stamped viciously upon the serpent of deism whenever opportunity offered. Such labors were, however, only part of the routine of editing the *Eagle*. Bunce reserved his full strength for the missionary movement, become by the spring of 1824 little short of a craze. Bunce could not understand the sudden, passionate interest of his erstwhile sensible Puritan neighbors in the heathen who dwelt in the remote parts of the earth. He felt that it was quite bad enough for women to squander their substance on leghorn hats and Canton crepes but that it became a matter for serious action when they attempted to seduce their husbands into donating hard-earned money for the purchase of pants and petticoats for worthless savages. Bunce felt called upon to smite this "newly discovered Christian duty" with all his strength.

He read in the *Religious Intelligencer* Timothy Stone's increasing lists of "female" benevolent societies. Then Bunce celebrated one of his own discovery: "The Female Bed-Bug Society; Mrs. Sally Pillow, president; Miss Amelia Bedcord, secretary."[2] He stumbled upon evidence that the missionary movement was boring into masonry, an organization of enormous prestige, and was informed that the Hiram Lodge in New Haven had, at an enthusiastic meeting, transformed itself into a missionary society for the conversion of Jews. A sharp editorial in the *Eagle* brought a recantation from the New Haven brothers. Bunce discovered in the *Missionary Herald* that an overzealous friend of missions was recommending "that 'the natural magic of experimental philosophy,' such as electricity—burning of gas—fireworks—sky-rockets, etc., be used before the Hindoos, Indians, and other heathen, to supply the place of miracles, to make them believe in christianity." Bunce was outraged at the suggestion that fraud be used to advance the true faith. It was, however, an episode occurring at Cornwall on January 24, 1824, that roused the *Eagle's* editor to the effort of his life.

In 1823 John Ridge, Cherokee, and cousin to Elias Boudinot, had left the Cornwall school to return to his home in the southern mountains. His father, Major Ridge, was a planter and slave owner who symbolized his acceptance of American civilization by giving his son the best education possible. While at Cornwall young Ridge had fallen

[2] *Ibid.*, June 30, 1823.

in love with Sarah Bird Northrup, daughter of the steward of the school. The girl's family objected to the marriage partly on the ground that the Indian, who was hobbling about on crutches, was not in good health. The Northrups finally agreed that, if Ridge after a year in which to get well should return to Cornwall without his crutches, they would give their consent. In January, 1824, a coach driven by a liveried slave rolled into the little village beneath Colt's Foot Mountain. It bore not only John Ridge but his dignified father. Major Ridge, tall and stately and dressed in the fashion of the time, made an impression upon the Cornwall Yankees. After her marriage Sarah Northrup became mistress of a plantation in the Cherokee country.

Long before the couple had reached the southern mountains, however, Isaiah Bunce had trained his heaviest artillery on the Foreign Mission School. "This subject of INTERMARRIAGES with the Indians and blacks of the missionary school at Cornwall now begun—and of this particular marriage is... not a subject for irony," wrote the *Eagle's* editor. "The affliction, mortification and disgrace, of the relatives of the young woman, who is only about sixteen years old, are too great for that.... To have her thus marry an Indian and taken into the wilderness among savages, must indeed be a heart rending pan[g] which none can realize except those called to feel it. We forbear to mention their names, or the name of her who has thus made herself a *squaw,* and connected her ancestors to a race of Indians. But her conduct, or the conduct of the Indian, her *sanup* or of her mother... is not so much a cause of wonder. It is, and will, it is believed on examination be found to be the fruit of the *missionary spirit,* and caused by the conduct of the clergymen at that place and its vicinity, who are agents and superintend the school. And though we shrink from recording the name of the female thus throwing herself into the arms of an Indian yet, 'daring to do all that may become a man or a christian,' we hesitate not to name those believed to be either mediately or immediately the cause of the unnatural connection; they are, Rev. Dr. Lyman Beecher, Rev. Timothy Stone, Rev. Charles Prentice, Rev. Joseph Harvey, and Rev. Herman Daggett. ... And the relatives of the girl, or the people of Cornwall, or the public at large, who feel indignant at the transaction, some of whom have said that the girl ought to be publicly whipped, the Indian hung, and the mother drown'd, will do well to trace the thing to its true cause, and see whether the men above named, or their system, are not the authors of the transaction as a new kind of *missionary machinery*."[8]

The missionary gentlemen who, as agents, managed the school were stunned. Recovering themselves they hastened with undignified alacrity to warn Connecticut Christians to limit their interest to the immortal souls of the heathen. They condemned miscegenation and forbade any further marriages at Cornwall across the race line. There were some difficulties in making the doctrine of race pride conform to the spirit of the "meek and lowly Jesus," but Lyman Beecher and Timothy Stone were men equal to the emergency.

※

The uproar at Cornwall subsided, but Bunce had only begun to fight. He was spurred to new efforts by the cheers of a gallery of new subscribers. In March he republished the article on "Intermarriages" and wrote a new attack upon the school. "Have not the females in that place been

[8] *Ibid.*, March 22, 1824.

seen to ride and walk out with them [the pupils of the Mission School] arm in arm, by night and by day—spend evenings with them — invite them to tea-parties—correspond with them by letters—and this by some who there called themselves the first, in short receiving them as the most favored gallants, and beaux, and the topknot of gentry; while the young men of the town, poor white boys, were often cast into the shade by their colored and tawny rivals? And this is known to more or less of the above named clergy and guardians of the school.... A gentleman from there since this took place, informs us that three other marriages with these natives, were supposed to be in treaty...."[4]

The young men in Cornwall considered themselves insulted. Had they lived in another section, they might have dragged the offending editor from his office and given him a dress of tar and feathers. In the South such stinging words would almost inevitably have led to an affair with pistols. But the young Puritans of Cornwall could think of no better way to salve their feelings than to hold a meeting.

"At a meeting of the Bachelors of 'Cornwall Valley' regularly convened, and held at the place appointed, with open doors on the 26th day of June, 1824, Mr. Rufus Payne, jun. was called to the chair, and John C. Lewis was chosen clerk; after which the annexed preamble and resolutions were drawn up, and unanimously adopted.

"Whereas Mr. Isaiah Bunce, the Editor of the Litchfield *Eagle* has frequently asserted in his paper, that the young ladies of this place show an undue partiality toward the members of the Foreign Mission School, and has frequently

[4] *Ibid.*

insinuated that we are thus cast in the shade, and eclipsed by the intervention of these our tawny rivals: —

"And whereas, the said Mr. Bunce has trained the bird which he calls the 'Eagle' to stretch its pitiful wings with scarce a feather to cover their leanness, over the conditions of the 'poor white boys of Cornwall Valley'; . . .

"Therefore, Resolved: That though we are single men . . . we do not fear that exportations to the wilderness, nor imputed partiality on the part of the young ladies here, towards the members of the Foreign Mission School, will render importation necessary, or compel us, Isaac-like, to go out of town for female helpers.

"Resolved: That though we feel no spirit of boasting in this case, and though we do not profess to be 'ladies' men,' still we spurn at the intimation that we have been cast into the shade, by our rivals, white or tawny. . . ."[5]

Colonel Benjamin Gold read carefully the Bunce attack. He was the father of two marriageable daughters. Because of his interest in the Mission School its pupils had many times been in his house. His family, sons and daughters alike, had corresponded with Cherokee Indians in the southern mountains. Benjamin Gold, thoroughly angry, bestirred himself to defend the good name of the school and of his own family. Together with seven other heads of Cornwall families he prepared a letter to the *American Eagle* requesting that it be published.

"Mr. Bunce: We, whose names are subscribed to this communication, are the heads of families, and have lived in the immediate vicinity of the Foreign Mission School, ever since its establishment. . . . For some time past, there have

[5] *Ibid.*, September 27, 1824.

Above: *Cornwall Village in 1838.*—Below: *Goshen, Connecticut, and the Road from Cornwall to Litchfield.* Both from *Connecticut Historical Collections*, 1838. Drawn by John Warner Barber

been frequent assertions in the paper of which you are the publisher, that there is a kind of intercourse subsisting between the families in the 'valley of Cornwall,' and the 'foreign scholars' which is highly improper.... With the best opportunity to know the truth in this case, we fully believe that such assertions as have appeared in your paper upon this subject are not *facts;* we deny that they are facts; and, in our turn, assert that they are *base fabrication.* And that the public may judge for themselves, upon the strength of evidence well attested, we invite you, sir, and we do it with the utmost cheerfulness, to tell the public the names of those persons from whom you claim to have heard the reports, the truth of which we here deny. If it be true that fifteen or twenty men from this town and some of them of 'family, probity, and standing,' have stated these things to you, doubtless they will not fear the avowal of their names. Probity will not fear to meet and shake hands with truth, in open day."[6]

Bunce did not have the sportsmanship to publish or to answer the letter. In August it finally saw the light in the *Connecticut Journal* of New Haven. The denial had barely reached the *Journal's* readers when Harriet Gold asked her father's permission to marry Elias Boudinot, who had sometime since returned to the Cherokee country.

[6] *Connecticut Journal,* August 10, 1824.

8

Fighting Against God

IN the autumn of 1824 a shadow fell across the house of Benjamin Gold. Harriet, now nineteen years old, a favorite of the village, and the idol of the family, hovered between life and death. The rooms were stilled; Swift, the fourteen-year-old baby of the household, was compelled to hold his animal spirits in leash. Catherine, an older sister of Harriet, minded the sick room and many times a day smoothed out the bright designs of the patchwork quilt upon the bed. She had already helped her mother store the wool in the attic; its spinning and weaving must await a more favorable time. Dr. Samuel Gold, a nephew of Benjamin, came as he felt his visits needed and prescribed to the best of his ability. But the knowledge of diseases and their cures possessed by even the greatest physicians in that day was fragmentary. The medicines which the good doctor left on the high bureau were almost as likely to harm as to help the patient.

Days passed and no change for the better in the patient appeared to bring cheer to those who ministered and waited. Word of the illness went out of the family—to Mary who had married General D. B. Brinsmade, and who now lived in the neighboring town of Washington; to Abby who was the wife of the Reverend Cornelius B. Everest, of Windham; and to Flora who, less than a year before, had married young Herman Vaill, and who was now settled at Millington. The sons were still at home or lived in Cornwall. Stephen, who was four years older than Harriet and particularly devoted to her, hurried in at night from the barn, his boots smelling of the stable, to inquire anxiously the latest word from the sick chamber. The Gold family hoped and prayed.

Eleanor Gold had just passed her sixtieth birthday when the sickness of her daughter added to her cares. The approach of death to her household was not a new experience for her. In her girlhood at Cornwall she had heard the excited talk in the village when a British raid in the Revolution penetrated as near to her home as Ridgefield. She had watched the men of Cornwall shoulder their muskets and march away to help stop Burgoyne when, with a powerful army and a horde of Indians, he advanced down the Hudson valley not far to the west. She had heard the terrifying story of the murder of young Jane M'Crea by one of Burgoyne's savages. In 1786, three years after the close of the Revolution, she had seen her firstborn, a daughter who had lived but four days, laid to rest in the cemetery. Two and a half years later a second daughter (and the third child) was born dead. In 1809 still another daughter, named for herself, passed away at the age of nineteen. In all, the names of fourteen children, eight daughters and six sons, were inscribed in the family Bible. She was forty-four when the last baby came. The graves on the little hill within sight of her house bound her to the soil where her father and grandfather had lived before her. The life of Eleanor Gold, deeply rooted in a community which changed but slowly, was, in a sense, typical of that of the Litchfield hills. Only once did she journey far from their shadows. From them, perhaps, she derived that strength of mind and body which enabled her to play a part in the Cornwall scene to the eve of the Civil War. In 1858, the year in which Lincoln debated Douglas in distant Illinois, she was gathered to her fathers at the age of ninety-two leaving more than one hundred descendants behind her. The crisis of her life, however, came in 1824 in the edge of winter when she looked into the wan face of Harriet. Slowly in the minds of Eleanor and Benjamin Gold the idea took form that they, perhaps, were responsible for the fact that their daughter was at the brink of death.

Harriet's sickness had reopened a question which the deacon considered closed—which he himself had painfully closed but a few weeks ago. Benjamin Gold remembered well the Cherokee youth called Elias Boudinot who, two or three years past, had spent four years at the Cornwall Mission School and had left to take a course at Andover Theological Seminary. Both Harriet and her brother, Franklin, had kept up a correspondence with him after he had returned to his people. Flora and Harriet, moreover, had exchanged letters with a Cherokee girl named Catherine. Doubtless the parents took a warm interest in this correspondence with a strange people who lived in the southern mountains. They, perhaps, smiled a little at Harriet's declared ambition to become a missionary. The young men of the Litchfield hills would have to be reckoned with before that could happen. Then, in the autumn of 1824, Harriet brought consternation to her father and mother by calmly asking permission to marry Elias Boudinot. Her sister, Mary Brinsmade, has told the story. "When H. had come to her conclusion in her own mind—she brought the subject before her parents—for she had no idea of acting without their consent—They had previously felt that marriages of this kind were not sinful—and now they had a severe trial in the case of their beloved daughter—merely to part with her was like breaking their heart-strings—and they brought up every argument which has since been brought forward to dissuade her and prevent the connection."[1]

Harriet's request was kept a profound secret even from the other members of the household while Eleanor and Benjamin Gold set about giving their daughter some instruction in New England common sense. Perhaps it was while they cleaned the pewter and the dishes of blue china that Harriet and her mother talked. There was sympathy in the elder woman's manner; she herself had been engaged at nineteen and married at twenty. Times had changed for the better since those hard first years after the war. But a woman's lot was still hard. Her tasks were heavy and were never done. There was water to draw and carry, meals to prepare, thread to spin, cloth and carpets to weave, and clothes — endless clothes—to make for a growing family. Forty years of married life had brought little rest to Eleanor Gold. Fortunate was the woman who won a considerate husband. The custom of the day made man the master and demanded that the wife yield obedience. Divorce was unthinkable. The good Lord knew that there was risk enough in marrying a man from the Litchfield hills. But an Indian! The mind of Eleanor Gold could not encompass the thought.

To the counsel of experience the girl opposed the faith of idealism. She trusted Boudinot. She longed to aid him in the work of instructing his people in Christian civiliza-

[1] The entire chapter is written from the *Vaill Mss.*

tion. In her short life she had heard much of extending the Kingdom of God to the heathen, of making the gospel shine in dark lands. The call from Macedonia seemed addressed peculiarly to her. The workers in the vineyard were few and there was need of haste. Had not Elias written only the year before that his people were dying of consumption, adding, "Perhaps ... Cherokee Nation is destined to fall by this Instrument of Death." God did not forbid marriages between red and white. In this case such a union would further His holy cause.

Benjamin Gold listened, one suspects, with little patience to the pleading of his daughter. He frankly had no desire for mixed-blood grandchildren. Perhaps he pictured the Cherokees as like the wretched remnant of the Scatacook tribe who still lived in the Housatonic valley not many miles below Cornwall. To be, as was Benjamin Gold, a successful merchant-farmer and a deacon of the first church in Cornwall was to occupy a position of dignity and influence. The fact that he had married two of his daughters to Congregational clergymen was, in itself, evidence of the social standing of his family. What would his two Yale-bred brothers think if a niece of theirs should marry an Indian? Harriet's own brothers and sisters would be shamed by the union she sought. The community would condemn it, although that was not a matter of supreme consequence to the son of Hezekiah Gold. Benjamin added a father's advice to the mother's counsel. But Harriet refused to budge. She too inherited the spirit of independence of the preacher who had found peace only in his grave on the near-by hill.

When argument and persuasion failed, Benjamin Gold fell back upon his prerogative as head of the house. One day in early autumn he composed a message to Elias Boudinot. The mail coach bore it away. It forbade the marriage. A little later Harriet collapsed before the onset of a disease which bore her swiftly to the brink of death.

The sleepy peace of Cornwall making its last preparations for the long, cold winter contrasted strangely with the tumult that stirred within the heart of Benjamin Gold. His reason told him that his decision had been wise and right. But a growing fear gripped him that he was fighting against God. Perhaps it was late at night in front of the great open fireplace whose flames lighted the dark corners of the living room that this aging man and his wife talked through their problem. Their God was one who ruled the affairs of men by His especial providence. They never doubted that He had followed every step of their course in dealing with Harriet's affair. Perhaps her sickness, which followed so soon upon the letter to Boudinot, was His warning to them. Perhaps, if their hearts remained stone, He would punish them by taking from them their dearest possession. Day after day they had prayed for Harriet's recovery—and her strength had continued to fail. Their petitions at the foot of the Mercy Seat had been worse than unanswered.

Their daughter, Mary, has told what happened. "Our parents felt ... that they might be found fighting against God—and some time during H's sickness they told her they should oppose her no longer, she must do what she thought best—Another letter accordingly sent to B. which he afterward acknowledged with gratitude as having reached him sooner than the one in which their opposition and refusal were expressed though their refusal was sent on several weeks first—Our parents thought it best not to tell the rest of the family at that time—as, in their opinion our opposition would do no good—and H. was in a delicate state of health—and they thought she could not bear it. Another reason why they did not tell us was—if this thing should ever take place it would not soon—perhaps in the providence of God, never—They did what they thought was their duty."

When winter snowbanks blocked the road from Cornwall to Goshen, Benjamin Gold rejoiced in the slowly returning health of his daughter. But his shoulders were bowed; he had saved her only to lose her in a singularly cruel manner. How hard and inexplicable, sometimes, are the ways of the Almighty! Perhaps, at times, unconsciously the deacon stiffened himself to meet the storm he knew must soon break upon him.

9

The Smoke of Their Torment

THE spring of 1825 was a difficult season for the Gold family. But there was no change in the routine of life. When the fields became green, the livestock was turned out to pasture. The sheep were sheared and the wool stored. Catherine, tired out by Harriet's illness, drove to Millington to visit Herman Vaill and her sister, Flora. The Vaills had a new baby girl. Harriet's illness had prevented Colonel Gold from sending to Flora the various articles of household equipment with which he was wont to provide his daughters when they married. The carpet which the Gold women were weaving for the Vaills had long hung untouched in its loom. Upon Catherine's return the spinning of the new wool would begin.

Concealed by the humdrum of life, apprehension harassed the minds of Eleanor and Benjamin Gold. They could see that the marriage of Sarah Northrup to John Ridge had nearly wrecked the Mission School. They were aware that, ever since that event, the agitated agents had lost no opportunity to explain that none of the parties involved in the affair were professing Christians and that they could not, therefore, be expected to take a deep interest in the Lord's work. Deacon Gold, perhaps, shared the common belief that the alliance had been instigated by Mrs. Northrup as a result of an abnormal interest in mixed marriages.

Against such a background Benjamin and Eleanor Gold had no illusions regarding the consequences of Harriet's decision. Their burden was made heavier by their loyalty to the school and the cause of which it was a part. Perhaps they now realized for the first time how deeply the Foreign Mission School had entered into their family life binding through loyalty to its cause the tribe of Gold more closely together. Ruggles Gold had prepared the way for the outpost of the Kingdom. Benjamin from the beginning had been an unwearying supporter. General Brinsmade, the husband of Mary Gold, was one of the agents of the institution. The school had brought Herman Vaill to Cornwall as instructor. As the weeks went by Benjamin and Eleanor postponed their announcement until Harriet should be fully recovered.

General Daniel Bourbon Brinsmade[1] held much the same position in the village of Washington that Benjamin Gold occupied in Cornwall. Both men were merchant-farmers. They were colleagues for several sessions in the General Assembly. In the state militia Gold was a colonel and Brinsmade a general. Both were deacons. Both were sincerely interested in the Foreign Mission School of which Brinsmade was an agent. Both men had virtually exhausted the possibilities of position and preferment, outside the professions, offered by an almost purely agricultural civilization. In the spring of 1825 they came to grips with one of the most difficult of social problems, marriage across the race line. The thought of both men was cast in the Puritan mold.

[1] A manuscript history of three members of the Brinsmade family, including the General, was prepared by a descendant and may be found in the Gunn Memorial Library at Washington, Connecticut.

Mary Gold was General Brinsmade's second wife. The difference between their ages is suggested by the fact that she was present as a child at his first wedding. In her first letter to her husband after their marriage she began in the formal style of the period, "Honored Sir." Mary was a quiet, conservative, and affectionate person; the General a tall, slender, nervous man, one of those Yankees whose restless energy and determined will made New England such a force in early nineteenth century America. His position on the Board of the Mission School compelled Brinsmade to make frequent trips to Cornwall. In the spring of 1825 he sensed that something was amiss. Doubtless Mary told him of her mother's strange remarks about Harriet. He finally learned the truth. Stephen Gold, in a letter to the Vaill family, narrated what action Brinsmade took. "The dye is cast, Harriet is gone, we have reason to *fear*. . . . Last tuesday Mr. Brinsmade made his suspicions known to the Board, and it made them (as he expressed it) 'as white as sheets'—Mr. Stone rose up and said it was a lie, but upon hearing Mr. B reasons, his mouth was stop'd. . . . Words cannot, no—let imagination *only express*, the feelings of my heart."[2]

Three days after the meeting of the agents the Reverend Joseph Harvey of Goshen, one of their number, called on Benjamin and Eleanor Gold. Speaking with the authority of a clergyman, he demanded to know if these parents had given their consent to the union mentioned by General Brinsmade. He was told the circumstances and informed that the matter lay entirely in Harriet's hands. The Sunday following he preached at Cornwall. No doubt his glance rose from that peaceful and unsuspecting congregation to

[2] *Vaill Mss.*

Harriet sitting in the choir as he thought of the secret which she harbored. Before he drove away on that quiet June Sunday, a long letter of his composing was handed to the young singer. It was an ultimatum to be answered within three days. The reply would immediately be submitted to a special meeting of the Board of Agents. If Harriet should give up her Indian, the agents would enjoin secrecy and the affair would never be known. If she refused, they would publish banns in the manner which seemed to them most fitting.

Harriet faced her decision alone. She understood the consequences of the step she was about to take. She had already had a stormy session with Stephen and had left her brother raging that he would murder the Indian if he ever set foot in Cornwall. She prayed. The answer to her petition was a strengthening of her conviction that her course was the only righteous one for her. She replied quietly to the Reverend Joseph Harvey that she intended to be a missionary and that she proposed to carry on her work as the wife of Elias Boudinot.

Lyman Beecher rode over to Cornwall for the special meeting of the agents. With mounting anger he listened to the reading of Harriet's letter. It was unendurable to be so flouted. The situation was desperate. The girl and her family must be publicly branded. It was doubtful if even the most drastic action would save the school. The agents issued on June 17 a special report in which were published the banns of Harriet Gold and Elias Boudinot.[8] "We the undersigned, being a part of the Agency of the Foreign Mission School, and having heretofore stated to the public

---

[8] The copy of this report received by Herman Vaill is in the *Vaill Mss.* Another copy may be found in the Cornwall library.

Harriet Gold Boudinot
From an oil portrait; artist unknown

that we believed no repetition of marriage connexion between any who have been members of the Foreign Mission School, and any female of the vicinity was to be expected ... now feel it to be our duty as honest men, to say to the public, that we have recently become acquainted with the fact, that a negociation for a marriage has been carried on secretly between Elias Boudinot a young Cherokee, who left the school with a good character, almost three years since, and has never returned, and Harriet R. Gold of this village; and that this negociation which has been carried on by secret and covered correspondence, has now become a settled engagement between the parties. In closing this communication we feel ourselves bound to say, that after the unequivocal disapprobation of such connexions, expressed by the Agents, and by the christian public universally; we regard those who have engaged in or accessory to this transaction, as criminal; as offering insult to the known feelings of the christian community: and as sporting with the sacred interests of this charitable institution. For those who have been guilty of this outrage upon public feeling, we can offer no apology; all we have to request is that the christian public will not condemn the innocent with the guilty: nor associate in their just censure, those who have been laboring to prevent this evil, with those who have thus induced it. Let the blame fall where it justly belongs. ... Lyman Beecher, Timothy Stone, Joseph Harvey, Philo Swift, Agents of the School." So Lyman Beecher sought to annihilate a girl whose concept of the good life did not agree with his.

The agents' printed pronouncement fell like a bomb in Cornwall. Excitement was intense. Groups of excited villagers assembled and dispersed only to assemble again. The word passed along the street that something must be done—that something would be done. Fearing violence Gold took Harriet by night to the house of a friend where she remained in hiding. Her window overlooked the green, and from her chamber she watched Cornwall give itself up to anger. Harriet herself has described the ceremony in which she was burned in effigy.

"In the evening our respectable young people Ladies and Gentlemen convened on the plain to witness and approve the scene and express their indignation. A painting had before been prepared representing a beautiful young Lady and an Indian; also on the same, a woman, as an instigator of Indian marriages. ... The church bell began to toll one would certainly conclude, speaking the departure of a soul. Mr. John C. Lewis and Mr. Rufus Payne carried the corpse and Brother Stephen set fire to the barrel of tar—or rather funeral pile. The flames rose high, and the smoke ascended—some said it reminded them of the smoke of their torment which they feared would ascend forever. My heart truly sang with anguish at the dreadful scene."[4]

The granddaughter of Hezekiah Gold did not waver. She was a Puritan mystic. Many times in her testament she had read the words written for those in distress. "Blessed are ye, when men shall revile you, and persecute you, and say all manner of evil against you falsely, for my sake. Rejoice and be exceeding glad: for great is your reward in heaven: for so persecuted they the prophets which were before you."

[4] *Vaill Mss.*

Soon after the affair on the green, Harriet opened her heart to Flora and Herman Vaill. "Yes it is so—the time has come when your Sister Harriet is already published to an *Indian*. If you have seen Mr. Stone's quarterly report you have seen our names and intentions. Pen cannot describe nor language express the numerous and trying scenes through which I have passed since you left us—But I trust I have had that support through them all, which the world could not give. Never before did I so much realize the worth of religion—and so much pity those, who, in time of trouble, were without this inestimable treasure. I have seen the time when I could close my eyes upon every earthly object and look up to God as my only supporter, my only hope—when I could say with emotion I never felt before, to my heavenly Father, 'other refuge have I none, so I helpless hang on thee.'

"I know that I appear at present to stand alone, the publick, 'good people and bad,' are against me—I cannot say that all are against me—there are many who are still my friends, but the excitement at present is such that they dare not have it known that they are on my side. You can have no idea of the scenes we have witnessed the week past. Yes, in this Christian land. The members of the M.S. many of them said it was more than they ever knew among the heathen. . . . [Mother] is almost worn out. She feels as though her children had no tenderness for her and instead of comforting her were ready to fill up her cup of affliction till it is more than running over. . . . I fear Brother Stephen has, to *prevent* a scandal brought a real scandal upon himself which cannot easily be wiped off—Even the most unprincipled say, they never heard of anything so bad even among the heathen as that of burning a sister in effigy—

Tomorrow eve is appointed for another meeting what will be done I know not. The Lord reigns—and I often repeat these comforting words 'Through waves and clouds and storms, He gently clears the way, we [wait] on his time—so shall this night, soon end in joyous day.' "

On the Sunday following the demonstration on the green, Mary Stone requested the young ladies who sang in the choir to wear white with a piece of black crepe on the left arm for Harriet who, until that day, had been one of their number.

10

The Tribe of Gold

GENERAL Daniel Bourbon Brinsmade seethed with rage.[1] On the twenty-ninth of June his agitated quill set to paper a call to battle addressed to Herman Vaill. "You have doubtless heard that the Cornwall business is all before the publick the agents have published the thing to the world. ... I shall do all in my power to prevent her getting away but expect it will be in vain. ... Our parents have long since given their written consent to the union thro Harrietts craftiness by making them believe she should die if she did not have her Indian last winter. I have not words to express my indignation at the whole proceeding—the whole family are to be sacrificed to gratify if I may so express it the animal feelings of one of its number—And lo! the whole is clothed in the garb of religion *they could not fight against God—is the reply*—I think the brothers and sisters are in duty bound to address their parents on this subject with suitable but decided disapprobation of the transaction. ... Cornwall is in great turmoil."

Cornwall valley resounded to the din of gossip. Rumors darted here and there like bees around an overturned hive. Sooner or later the reports all came to the home of the Reverend Timothy Stone. Mary Stone became an oracle

---

[1] This chapter has been built up entirely from the *Vaill Mss*.

at whose feet even the agents sat. The image of a plot took form. Benjamin, Eleanor, and Harriet Gold had long planned in secret the "Indian connexion." During all those months while, in fact, they were undermining the foundations of the Foreign Mission School they were publicly and hypocritically playing the rôle of its friends and supporters. Mary Stone whispered in the ear of the Reverend Joseph Harvey, A.M., of Goshen. Whereupon Joseph Harvey harnessed his horse and, riding to Millington, whispered in the ear of the Reverend Herman Vaill. Herman Vaill, always the man to heed the call of duty, wrote Harriet Gold a letter. When he had expressed himself to his satisfaction, he had composed nearly five thousand words. He was rather proud of the effort; he spoke of having it published. He investigated Harriet's proposed marriage against a background of Puritan theology.

Herman's homiletical training stood him in good stead. With a proper respect for logic he began at the beginning of his argument. He had long known and sympathized with Harriet's desire to become a missionary. If the "Great Head of the Church" had called her, her Christian friends and relatives must cheerfully, though sadly, have given their parting blessings and "the Farewell." "But there is a wide difference between going among the heathen by the call, the leading of Providence; and going among them merely because we will to go. There is a wide difference between going, because we love the cause of Christ, and have a single eye to his glory; and going because we love another object; and have a selfish inducement." Vaill hastened to explain that he did not consider mixed marriages criminal. Nor did he have any objection to Boudinot, whom he knew well. Herman, however, would have thought more of the Indian if he had not considered it "necessary that he should marry a white woman."

Wherein, then, lay the sin which Harriet was planning to commit? Her proposed marriage would "annihilate" the Foreign Mission School. The object of that institution was not to bring about a mixture of races but rather "it was to civilize, and to Christianize the heathen; and to prepare them to become, like Thomas Hopoo, the sober, chaste, kind husbands of wives from among their own people; and to qualify them to become the enlightened, converted, and obedient subjects of the kingdom of Christ." The closing of the Mission School would, moreover, "injure the interests of missions, in our churches generally." "Less of a missionary spirit will prevail; fewer missionary sermons will be preached;—Less money will be contributed;—and ... more of the heathen will be lost."

Herman was warming to his subject. If Harriet should marry Elias Boudinot, many a poor heathen's soul that might otherwise have been saved would languish in Hell. "Beware then how you suffer yourself to hope that God will defend the Mission School, while you take measures to overthrow it. — He can defend it if he pleases — but He works by means;—and we are to take heed what we do to render these means unavailing.—The Church is safe; and the people of Christ, wherever they are, shall come to Him. Should you become the instrument of the school's destruction, God will cause the heathen to hear his word through some other channel—'Deliverance will arise to them from another place';—but remember the word, 'but thou, and thy father's house, shall be destroyed.' " Here Herman achieved a dialectical triumph. He succeeded in having his omnipotent God save the heathen anyway while damning Harriet and her family for overthrowing the Mission School which He elected not to rescue. Flushed with this success the young theologian hurried on to his climax. "And thus you must take into account, not only the injury done to the cause at large, but also all the tears of the people of God, and all the dishonour thrown upon His cause, and His friends, by the occasion you thus give the enemy to blaspheme.—But infinitely more than all this, you will bring dishonour upon the Saviour. His church and his cause are dear to Him as the apple of his eye,—and if you wound them, you will by the same stroke open his wounds afresh. You profess to be his disciple. He expects to see his disciples engaged supremely in the interests of his Kingdom. For this Kingdom he has bled; and O Harriet, He has already bled enough; and should you go on, well might the Redeemer say, in view of the wounds which you would thus give him, 'They are those with which I am wounded in the house of my friends.' "

Master of the field after having vanquished every counter-argument, Herman Vaill, Puritan, became censorious. "... all this has been going on with the knowledge, and at least the secret aid and approbation of your Parents; and this too, in the very face of your Mother's repeated protestations of ignorance, and of your Father's public affidavit; which all who have read will now turn against him, as evidence he has knowingly disguised the truth.... We shall feel for our aged Parents; for their sun is near his setting; and we fear that if you go, the sun of their Christian reputation is already set.... Do you hesitate? ... Do not go away like Cain and Judas; but come back like Peter.... Will you go? If you are a hypocrite, and designed for a reprobate, doubtless you will. But if you are a Christian, it must be you will listen, and regard the advice of friends, and the call of God and his church. As ever, your affectionate brother H. L. Vaill."

※

Weeks passed with no word from Cornwall. Then a letter posted in Washington came from Mary Brinsmade. Mary's letter, as well as that of Herman Vaill, expressed the mind of Puritanism. The two together give a fairly complete picture of Connecticut religious thought and attitude with respect to a difficult social problem. "I am unwilling to remain silent another week. I have had a multitude of conflicting emotions concerning our sister Harriet since we last saw each other, but my mind has at last become calm. . . . Harriet never appeared more interesting than she does at present. It is a time of great commotion in C. still Harriet is meek, though firm as the hills. . . . I opposed the thing till conscience repeatedly smote me, and now, I must acknowledge that I feel it my duty to be still—my feelings are in unison with the multitude of my christian friends who tell me to comfort Harriet. Some of the most consciencious and best informed christians in Washington think that some great good is to be brought about in these latter days by means of this event—Mr. Mason and several other clergymen in this region say, decidedly, that they think no one ought to oppose and distress H. now. . . . We complain of the *tendency* of this thing but let us not forget that we are shortsighted beings of a day. We have a great trial, and may we be enabled to exercise the spirit of Christ. . . . Let not *pride* have any hand in distressing us. . . . Permit me to tell you, my dear brother, that I was sorry to see some expressions which I saw in the latter part of the letter which

H. received from you last week—Our parents thought you said very hard things and very unjustly."

In the same mail Herman Vaill found a letter from Sister Mary's husband. It suggested that the general of all the cavalry of Connecticut had doubts of his ability to command his wife. "... There is high times in C.—and I expect nothing but that Fathers property will—You know his situation. ... Bunce has come out with a particular notice of the respectability of the family and all the *Indian's* brothers in law are mentioned except Br. Everest. I think he must consider himself slighted — how does Millington people like the idea of having a clergymen who is brother to an Indian. ... O, I am sick at heart."

A few weeks later Catherine Gold wrote to Vaill. "I believe it is not thought best by anyone that has seen your letter that you should publish it. Mary says unless you wish to disgrace yourself you must not publish it. ... Harriet said she thought your letter was a pretty candid one till nearly the close but she cannot put up with this."

The Reverend Herman Vaill was beginning to discover the cloth had less prestige within the family circle than he had supposed. He soon found a salve for his smarting pride in a letter from his brother-in-law, the Reverend Cornelius B. Everest of Windham, Connecticut, the husband of Abby Gold. The news of Harriet's affair had galvanized this man of God into action. "Depend upon it we are *steadfast, immovable* and almost continually *abounding* in our efforts to break up the Indian wedding. I wrote ... to E. B. which will be a *damper* if not a *death blow* to this business. I have written to brother Brinsmade; another to brother Hopkins —another to sister Katherine in answer to one just like the one she wrote to you. I wrote a letter mild and respectful but *High charged*. I have written to Uncles Thomas Ruggles Gold and Thomas Gold; and have an answer from uncle Ruggles stating that in complyance with my request he has written to his brother Benj'n 'pretty fully to endeavour to recall him from his devious courses back to the sentiments of his friends and connections.' I knew all you have stated about sister Mary ... But we are firm, and shall remain so whether the wind blows high or low. I cannot believe that the wedding will take place—I hope not. *Fighting ag't God*—I cannot endure such stuff. ... Stand firm. You need not fear about us. You may ever know where to find us ... Affectionately yours—C. B. Everest."

A little late Brother Cornelius became solicitous of Catherine's future. In view of the loss of prestige caused by the "Indian connexion," he suggested, "what are the prospects of the unmarried and unsettled children?" No young man had as yet appeared upon Catherine's horizon. If Catherine were apprehensive, her worries were short-lived. Six months did not pass before she became the bride of a widower possessed of ample means, a commendable character, and three children.

In September Herman Vaill opened, no doubt with some nervousness, a letter from Cornwall written in the well-known hand of Benjamin Gold. "Mr. H. L. Vaill—Sir— After a length of time we send you and Flory things we have provided—the sickness has been so great here that we could not send sooner—if you are thankful for them well—if not you will be unthankful—I saw the long letter you wrote Harriet—in which you throw out many things against her and me and my wife—about the Indian connection—which are altogether uncandid—unjust—and untrue

... to all of which I do not see fitt to make any lengthy reply at present—It is through pride and prejudice—that all this clamour has been raised *against Indians* and the least that can be said and done against Christian connections of any colour I believe to be best—our whol family which have been together this summer have become very harmonious on this subject . . . as you may yourself perceive —in very great hast I subscribe myself your Father and Friend Benj'n Gold."

11

Dawn

BENJAMIN and Eleanor Gold went on with the business of life. Harriet worked, a little wistfully, at her hope chest. Autumn passed and again the frozen ground was covered with snow. Herman Vaill, chastened by his rebuffs, wrote a letter of apology to the Cornwall Golds. January found Harriet writing Vaill, describing Catherine's wedding. "With pleasure I hasten to answer the letter we received from you yesterday. I have been for some time wishing to write and shall probably have time to write more than one girls letter—but as to Sister Catherine, in vain do you wish for another girls letter from her—I am now left an only daughter—and Sedgwick is the only brother I have left at home—Catherine is now in Sharon. She was married Christmas morning before meeting— The day was rainy, but the wedding very pleasant. . . . Catherine's carpet is now in the loom, and we shall try among us all to weave it. As soon as hers is out of the Loom Mrs. Brown will get in yours and I have long since by my own contrivance paid . . . for the weaving of yours. . . . Now what to tell you about myself I hardly know. . . . I hope to hear from my far distant friend before long and know how soon I shall go. My box is made and I am trying to fill it with something—have some presents for all which I am very grateful. . . . Sister Mary comes home very often and we have precious family visits. You have probably heard of Br. Everest's visit to Cornwall. [He came to see his aged mother and never entered the house of Benjamin Gold.] Many remarks are made—some will say —'Is this a minister of the gospel?' others 'Why I think ministers are worse than other folks' ... As for our part we are sorry Br. E. has given occasion for so many remarks. We fear he does not feel as a christian ought to feel —and we do sincerely pity Sister Abbey. ... I think she must be very unhappy and am sorry for her. You cannot think what precious interviews we four sisters ... [Harriet, Catherine, Mary, and Flora] do enjoy. We shall have but few more opportunities of praying and singing together here but we part with the blessed hope and expectation of meeting in that happier world where we shall reunite in perfect songs of praise which shall never cease. ... When I realize the parting with my dear Father, dear Mother, dear Sisters, and dear brothers and friends—the thought pierces my very heart, it is trying beyond description—still it is my desire to go."

March came. The day set for the wedding was near at hand. Boudinot was on his way northward. Herman Vaill wrote to Harriet. Painful experience during the last few months had taught the young divine many things concerning the nature of the good life. Those who accept the hypothesis that reserve is the foundation of New England character would do well to read his farewell note.

"Dear Sister Harriet R. Gold, whose Gold will shortly become dim—and to whom, I write now, with this appelation, probably for the last time. ... You know, dear Sister, you know I always loved you; and that difference of opinion with regard to the propriety and expediency of your contemplated connexion . . . has not abated my desire to see you happy and useful. I have the same affectionate, fraternal regard for you as ever; and hope that you will be the instrument of accomplishing much in behalf of that People whom I now suppose you consider your Nation. . . . Go, dear Sister, and if you have erred, beseech God to forgive you; go and in His cause, and in His strength, do all the good you can. And must we thus part? Am I never to see you more? Are you never more to see your dear sister and my dear wife; never to see our . . . little Catherine Harriet? It may be so. . . . My sister we shall remember you; we shall remember you at the Throne of Grace; and you will there remember us. Our request is that you would always write to us—once in 3 mo's and we will answer you as often. My kind regards, and best wishes, to Brother Boudinot, when he becomes your husband. Affectionately yours, H. L. Vaill—Farewell."

On March 28, 1826, Harriet Gold and Elias Boudinot were married at the home of Benjamin Gold. Stephen worked in the sawmill during the ceremony. He had long since ceased to threaten. A new minister at Goshen who had succeeded the Reverend Joseph Harvey performed the rites. The absence of Timothy Stone was not without significance. Because of the part he had played in Harriet's affair the tide of opinion of a changeable public was already running against him. Mournfully he witnessed in the autumn of this same year the closing of the doors of the Foreign Mission School. In May, 1827, he found himself dismissed from his pulpit by a hostile parish. Lyman Beecher left Connecticut to fight the battles of the Lord in eastern Massachusetts. "Father and Mother," wrote Flora

Vaill in 1825, "have sustained good character in this place too long to be overthrown by the agents or any other one."

Still fearing violence Benjamin and Eleanor Gold accompanied the Boudinots as far as Washington, Connecticut. There the girl of twenty-one bade farewell to her parents and struck out for herself. Her vision was bright before her. "I cannot but rejoice in prospect of spending my days among those despised people and, as the time draws near, I long to begin my work. I think I may reasonably expect many trials, hardships, and privations. May I never be disposed to seek my own ease any farther than is consistent with the greatest usefulness."

PART III
BROTHERHOOD OR FORCE

12

High Tower

DECEMBER, 1826, brought chill winds to the coves on the sides of Cohutta Mountain. The Cherokees prepared for cold winter months. But, even as the old year died, new life stirred in a tiny and somewhat dilapidated mission station known as High Tower and located in the edge of the uplands. Past the door of the cabin which housed the mission flowed the Etowah River. The High Tower windows looked out over the rich Conasauga valley. Thirty-five miles to the north, Spring Place mourned the passing of Brother John Gambold who, only in the previous month, had followed Sister Anna to the grave. High Tower had been established, some four years before, by a missionary of the American Board of Commissioners for Foreign Missions, the same Puritan society which had supported the Cornwall School and whose "Mission Rooms" were in Boston. When the founder of this mountain outpost had been called to other fields, the station had languished. On December 1, 1826, Elias and Harriet Boudinot came to High Tower to renew in that sector the war against heathendom.

The region about the station was familiar to Elias. Here lived his family and many of his childhood playmates. He was a prophet returning to his own country. By early January the building had been put in order and about a dozen scholars had been gathered. Elias was both missionary and schoolmaster. His course at Cornwall and his later study at Andover Theological Seminary made him one of the best educated men in the Cherokee Nation. The A.B.C.F.M. was fortunate to get an Indian of such attainments to renew the decayed work at High Tower. "The Mission find us and we have $20 pr month,"[1] Boudinot wrote to Herman Vaill. The post was to be for the winter only, for Elias had other and larger plans.

After three months with her husband's people Harriet was at last keeping house in her own home. Her days were crowded. There were many guests and, after the beginning of the new year, the scholars had to be boarded. But she was full of hope and enthusiasm. She snatched time from her household duties to write a long letter to Herman and Flora and to answer those questions which she knew filled their minds.

"My Cherokee father often reminds me of my own Father by his cheerfulness and I think is remarkable for his amiable, kind and affectionate disposition. Sister M[ary] says he used often to speak of me before I came here—said I was going to leave all my friends to come and do them good, and they must love me a great deal—and both he and My Dear Cherokee Mother frequently say that I am like an own child to them. Mother is a very feeble woman—but never idle if she is able to be off her bed. She cuts and makes all the clothes for the family except the coats for the men. She is remarked by all who know her for her amiable kind and friendly disposition. Our oldest Br. named Stand is a young man about 21—has a decent education, and is much esteemed in the Nation. Nancy is our eldest sister. She is 19

---

[1] Vaill Mss.

or 20, not a woman of her age smarter for business. She is also amiable and kind in her disposition—a member of the church at Hawies. Next is Br. Thomas. He attends school ... Next is Sister Mary—now living with Mr. Remley's family at Echota. She has always been a great favourite with me—is remarkably lively, has a good mind, and it will not be saying too much to say I know of no girl of her age and advantages superior to her. She wishes to write to Mother and probably will before long. Next is Betsey our youngest sister at school. She reads and spells well, is a very pretty girl. ... The next is John Alexander Petrie, formerly called Henry. He was selected by the Missionaries and named by the request of Mr. J. A. Petrie of Charleston, S. C. who wishes to give him a thorough English education. Mr. Boudinot received a letter a few weeks since from Miss Sarah H. Petrie. ... The youngest of all is a daughter and is yet a babe—name Susan. ... I love them all much—and I may say we love each other.

"You also wish to know what we have to eat. At Father Watie's we had coffee, Sugar, Tea, milk, Corn and wheat bread, Beef, Pork, Venison and an abundance of fowls—and I sometimes made puddings, pies and cakes. Butter, cheese, apple sauce, and pickles are not as plenty as they probably will be hereafter. At this place we have not a great variety—but do very well. ... I not only rise early enough to get my own food but sometimes for ten or fifteen besides. Now Sister Flora ... your family and work are insignificant compared with mine. Since we came here, until the last two weeks I had no assistance except Sister Betsey when out of school and our family has averaged most of the time 8 or 10. Christmas time we had several interesting meetings and company from abroad. For four days I had from ten to fifteen to wait upon. ... My love to all my friends. Visit our Parents often and do everything for their comfort. O my dear precious Mother, how shall we ever repay half her kindness to us Your Cherokee Sister."[2]

⚜

One of the December guests of the Boudinots was a missionary who rode over to High Tower from Brainerd, another station of the A.B.C.F.M. located near Lookout Mountain in Tennessee. Samuel Austin Worcester was an earnest young Puritan most of whose twenty-eight years had been spent in New England.[3] Behind him in his genealogical tree was an unbroken line of eight Congregational clergymen. After graduating from the struggling University of Vermont of which his uncle, Samuel Austin, was president, he had prepared himself for the mission field at Andover Seminary. In 1825 he took to Brainerd as his bride Ann Orr, who had been a schoolmate of Mary Lyon at one of the best girls' schools of the day. Ann Worcester remained in Tennessee while Samuel spent a fortnight at High Tower.

The young Vermonter's intellectual abilities had been one of the reasons for his being sent to Brainerd in the important Cherokee field. His superiors hoped that he would be able to master the language of those Indians, esteemed in mission circles to be as difficult as Chinese. Worcester found in Boudinot a tutor to train him in the Cherokee tongue. John Gambold to the end of his days could speak to the Indians only through interpreters. He had concentrated, therefore, on the bilingual mixed bloods. Worcester, unlike the Moravians, determined to get to

[2] *Ibid.*
[3] See Nevada Couch, *Pages from Cherokee Indian History as Identified with Samuel Austin Worcester* . . . (3d ed.; St. Louis, R. P. Stanley & Co., 1884).

the very core of Cherokee culture. After mastering the language he hoped to bring the red mountaineers into contact with the thought currents of the white man's world. On every hand he could see the progress of the Cherokees in material civilization. He dreamed of a comparable advance in the realms of mind and spirit.

After the New Englander had said goodbye to his hosts at High Tower, Elias Boudinot confided his impressions of his guest to Hermann Vaill. "Mr. Worcester ... spent some time with us—while here we commenced systematizing the Cherokee language and forming rules for the formation of tenses. I presume the Cherokee verbs are the most complicated in the world. ... You will form a slight idea of the almost infinite forms in the Cherokee verbs, when I tell you that we have discovered 29 tenses in the Indicative mode, in all the verbs, and 30 in some, and that in the verb *To tie,* there are not less than 178 forms, only in the present Tense indicative Mode. Mr. Worcester however proceeds rapidly in acquiring the language—he intends to preach in it—the blessings of God attend him."[4]

Almost the same post that took Boudinot's epistle northward carried a letter from Samuel Worcester to his Boston chief, Jeremiah Evarts. "I have more confidence in Boudinot as a translator than in any other: and, though I may be deceived, and some have greatly doubted, yet my spending near a fortnight in his family has given me quite a respect for his character. His appearance is that of one sincerely pious. He is beginning to speak in public meetings in his own language, and, I suspect, quite to the purpose. His wife, too, appears to me to possess in an uncommon degree such qualifications as are requisite for missionary

[4] *Vaill Mss.*

service."[5] So began a friendship between these red and white sons of Andover which remained unbroken so long as Elias Boudinot lived.

The friendship was the result of an intellectual partnership. The two undertook the task of translating into Cherokee selected books of the white man. They built frankly on foundations laid only a few years before by an Indian with a spirit and outlook akin to their own but whom, in all probability, they never saw. Two years before Worcester came to Brainerd Sequoyah left the southern mountains for the west and never returned. Sequoyah's great achievement throws light on the intellectual problems which Worcester and Boudinot confronted.

[5] Worcester to Evarts, January 8, 1827, in Worcester Mss. in library of Andover Theological Seminary.

13

Sequoyah

BOUDINOT'S work among the Cherokees rested on the corner stone laid by Sequoyah.¹ This man was born near Echota in the heart of the Cherokee country. His early life was shaped by the old tribal culture of the Little Men and the Immortals. He came to excel as a hunter and trader in furs. He had no schooling. Schools came to the Cherokees with the missionaries and Sequoyah was already a man when the Moravian brothers founded Spring Place. He never learned to speak, read, or write the English language. After 1800, however, he became increasingly conscious of the white man's civilization. It was penetrating the Cherokee country in the form of spinning wheels, looms, grist mills, and occasional smithies. Sequoyah was no conservative; he adjusted his life to the changing time. While continuing to hunt, he learned the art of the silversmith. Soon he was shaping from the white metal arm bands, gorgets, and a variety of other trinkets which his copper-colored neighbors desired. Sequoyah had a natural manual dexterity, a feeling for beauty, and an eye for business.²

[1] See Albert V. Goodpasture, "The Paternity of Sequoyah, the Inventor of the Cherokee Alphabet," *Chronicles of Oklahoma*, I, 121 ff.

[2] The familiar story of Sequoyah is told in George E. Foster, *Se-quo-yah* . . . (Tahlequah, Cherokee Nation, H. B. Stone, 1885). See also Grant Foreman, *Sequoyah* (Norman, University of Oklahoma Press, 1938). This is an excellent account.

But a strange discontent impaired his peace of mind. As early as 1809 he became impressed with the ability of white men, with whom he came into occasional contact, to make their thoughts stick to paper and so to preserve them. On the chase and in his smithy Sequoyah could not escape the feeling that the white man's trick was the explanation of his superiority. The grandson of Christopher Gist began to dream of marks on paper that would hold captive the fleeting spoken words of the Cherokees. A hunting accident in middle life made him a cripple and compelled him to depend more than ever upon his thoughts for the satisfactions of life. Sequoyah's was a mind which became aware that it was engulfed in night. He sensed the existence of light beyond the horizon which limited him. He set out to blaze a trail to the sun.

Groping for a way to visualize words, he experimented with pictographs. Unwittingly he started at the beginning of the trail which long before had led men to the discovery of writing. Sequoyah's tentative picture writing ran into hundreds of symbols. Then he found his progress blocked by the same complex verbs of which Boudinot and Worcester later complained. He discovered that a single such verb would require for its representation scores of different pictures. Sequoyah gave up his attempt to develop a picture writing and tried a different approach.

He broke up the words of the Cherokees into syllables and made the discovery that the syllable sounds of the language were surprisingly few in number. If he omitted those which began with the sound of "s," there were scarcely more than eighty. He conceived the idea of inventing a symbol for each syllable sound. He discarded pictures and imitated the Roman letters, meaningless to him, which he found in an old speller that he had acquired. Some letters he appropriated without change; others suggested new symbols which he invented. Perhaps the most brilliant aspect of the achievement was the use of the symbol for the hissing sound "s" as a true letter when placed before another character. By this device of simplification Sequoyah compelled eighty-three characters to transmit Cherokee thought. So thorough was his scholarship that later only three undesignated syllable sounds were discovered—perhaps by Sequoyah himself.

The first half of the nineteenth century in America saw the accomplishment of no more difficult intellectual achievement than that of the Cherokee silversmith. The syllabary immediately roused the admiration of Albert Gallatin, secretary of the treasury under Jefferson and pioneer American anthropologist. "When the first imperfect copy of the alphabet syllabary was received at the War Department," he commented, "it appeared incredible that a language known to be so copious should have but eighty-five syllables.... It would have taken but one step more for Se-quo-yah to have reduced the whole number of consonants to sixteen, and to have had an alphabet similar to ours—by giving to each consonant a distinct character. In practice, however, the superiority of Se-quo-yah's alphabet is manifest, and has been fully proved by experience. You must learn and remember eighty-five letters instead of twenty-five. But this once accomplished the education of the pupil is completed; he can read, he is perfect in his orthography without making it the subject of distinct study. The boy learns in a few weeks that which occupied two years of the time of our boys."[8]

[8] Quoted in Foster, *Se-quo-yah*, 103.

In 1821, the year before Elias Boudinot left Cornwall for Andover, Sequoyah was ready to announce the results of his investigations. Five years before he had been a prominent man in the tribe and had signed a treaty with his mark in 1816. Now he discovered that the Cherokee Council, which he approached, was reluctant to listen to him. No Indian could spend his time making strange marks on the bark of trees without being thought crazy. But messages sent back and forth in the presence of the Council between the scholar and his little daughter were too convincing to be ignored. The leaders of the Cherokees, half persuaded, arranged for a test. They selected a group of young men with sharp minds and sent them to Sequoyah's cabin. At the appointed time the chiefs assembled and subjected these students to the most rigid tests. When the meeting ended, the scholar was a tribal hero. A great feast was held in his honor and he listened to speeches of praise from the great ones of the nation. Sequoyah had matched the trick of the white man. He had opened a gate for the Cherokee people. Through it could be glimpsed a path leading ever upward until it was lost in shimmering dreams of Indian greatness.

Sequoyah realized that with the official acceptance of his syllabary by the Cherokee Nation his life had reached the end of a chapter. He determined that it should not be the end of the book. With the plaudits of his friends and neighbors sounding in his ears, he left forever the southern mountains and journeyed to Arkansas where in 1818 and 1819 some five thousand Cherokees had removed because they preferred the old free hunting life to the stuffy ways of civilization. To the western band of Cherokees Sequoyah taught his syllabary. Immediately the two branches of the tribe began to exchange ideas and information. In the midst of his western success the aging smith received from John Ross, the principal chief of the eastern Cherokees, a medal wrought in Washington out of the silver he knew so well in recognitition of his services to the Nation.

But still that strange discontent within him was not quieted. It became a yearning to achieve the unattainable. It robbed his declining years of peace. An old, half-forgotten tradition of the Cherokees told of a band which in antiquity had wandered into the distant land of Mexico and had never been heard of since. Death caught up with Sequoyah in the little Mexican settlement of the long lost Cherokees—still striving to make dreams come true.

14

A Press for the Cherokees

ELIAS BOUDINOT dreamt as boldly as Sequoyah. But his vision took him northward. On May 26, 1826, he stood in the pulpit of the First Presbyterian Church of Philadelphia to plead the cause of his people. It was the spring before he opened the school at High Tower. The Philadelphia address was one of many which he delivered on an extended tour. His object was to raise funds. To make his hearers understand the significance of his request he recounted the progress in civilization of his people.

"The Cherokee nation," he said to listeners some of whom had never heard of the tribe, "lies within the chartered limits of the states of Georgia, Tennessee, and Alabama. Its extent as defined by treaties is about 200 miles in length from East and West, and about 120 in breadth. ... The rise of these people in their movement toward civilization may be traced as far back as the relinquishment of their towns; when game became incompetent for their support, by reason of the surrounding white population. They then betook themselves to the woods, commenced the opening of small clearings, and the raising of stock; still however following the chase. Game has since become so scarce that little dependence for subsistence can be placed upon it. They have gradually and I could almost say universally forsaken their ancient employment. ... It cannot be doubted, however that there are many who have commenced a life of agricultural labour from mere necessity, and if they could, would gladly resume their former course of living. But these are individual failings and ought to be passed over. ...

"It is a matter of surprise to me, and must be to all those who are properly acquainted with the condition of the Aborigines of this country, that the Cherokees have advanced so far and so rapidly in civilization. But there are yet powerful obstacles, both within and without, to be surmounted in the march of improvement. The prejudices in regard to them in the general community are strong and lasting. The evil effects of their intercourse with their immediate white neighbors, who differ from them chiefly in name, are easily to be seen, and it is evident from this intercourse proceed those demoralizing practices which in order to surmount, peculiar and unremitting efforts are necessary. In defiance, however, of these obstacles the Cherokees have improved and are rapidly improving. ... At this time there are 22,000 cattle; 7,600 horses; 46,000 swine; 2,500 sheep; 762 looms; 1,488 spinning wheels; 172 wagons; 2,948 ploughs; 10 saw mills; 31 grist mills; 62 blacksmith shops; 8 cotton machines; 18 schools; 18 ferries; and a number of public roads. In one district there were, last winter, upward of 1,000 volumes of good books. ... On the public roads there are many decent Inns. ... Most of the schools are under the care and tuition of Christian missionaries, of different denominations, who have been of great service to the nation, by inculcating moral and religious principles into the minds of the rising generation. ... The missionaries have been encouraged by the proper authorities of the nation, their persons have been protected. ... Indeed it may be said with truth, that among no heathen people has the faithful minister of God experienced greater success, greater reward for his labour than in this. He is surrounded by attentive hearers, the words which flow from his lips are not spent in vain. ...

"There are three things of late occurence, which must certainly place the Cherokee nation in a fair light. ... First. The invention of letters. Second. The translation of the New Testament into Cherokee. And third, The organization of a Government. ...

"The translation of the New Testament, together with Guest's [Sequoyah's] mode of writing, has swept away that barrier which has long existed, and opened a spacious channel for the instruction of adult Cherokees. ... The Government though defective in many respects, is well suited to the condition of the inhabitants. As they rise in information and refinement, changes in it must follow, until they arrive at that state of advancement, when I trust they will be admitted into all the privileges of the American family. ... Polygamy is abolished. Female chastity and honor are protected by law. The Sabbath is respected by the Council during session. Mechanics are encouraged by law. The practice of putting aged persons to death for witchcraft is abolished and murder has now become a governmental crime. ...

"The Cherokees have thought it advisable that there should be established, a Printing Press and a Seminary of respectable character; and for these purposes your aid and patronage are now solicited. They wish the types, as expressed in their resolution, to be composed of English letters and Cherokee characters. Those characters have now become extensively used in the nation; their religious songs are written in them; there is an astonishing eagerness in people of all classes and ages to acquire a knowledge of them. ...

"When before did a nation of Indians step forward and ask for the means of civilization. ... With that assistance what are the prospects of the Cherokees? ... I can view my native country, rising from the ashes of her degradation, wearing her purified and beautiful garments, and taking her seat with the nations of the earth. I can behold her sons bursting the fetters of ignorance and unshackling her from the vices of heathenism. She is at this instant, risen like the first morning sun, which grows brighter and brighter, until it reaches its fulness of glory. ...

"There is, in Indian history, something very melancholy, and which seems to establish a mournful precedent for the future events of the sons of the forest. ... We have seen every where the poor aborigines melt away before the white population. ... We have seen, I say, one family after another, one tribe after another, nation after nation pass away; until only a few solitary creatures are left to tell the sad story of extinction. ... Must they perish? Must they all ... go down in sorrow to their grave? They hang upon your mercy as to a garment. Will you push them from you, or will you save them? Let humanity answer."[1]

The Philadelphians made their way slowly out of the church leaving a contribution behind. Boudinot continued his speaking tour. The money which he helped to collect purchased a printing press. While he was at High Tower, type was cast in Boston carrying Sequoyah's symbols. After

[1] Elias Boudinot, *An Address to the Whites* (Philadelphia, printed by W. F. Geddes, 1826).

much expenditure of time and effort the press and type were transported by way of the trader's paths over the mountains to the Conasauga valley, and the printing establishment was set up at New Echota. On February 21, 1828, appeared the first number of the first American Indian newspaper ever to be published. The *Cherokee Phœnix* bore the name of Elias Boudinot, editor.

15

New Echota

ELIAS BOUDINOT proved an enterprising editor. He wrote to Herman Vaill at the outset of the career of the new paper urging his brother-in-law to secure subscriptions for the *Phœnix*. The letter disclosed the dual objective of Boudinot. He hoped that his paper would keep the missionary-minded people of the North interested in Cherokee affairs while, at the same time, it brought current news to the isolated Indian. Boudinot was modest. "We have nothing to recommend our paper," he remarked to Vaill, "but novelty and our good intentions. We do not wish to be thought as striving to rival other papers of the day, by exhibiting to the public, learning, talents and information, for these we do not profess to possess. ... Our object is simple, and in our opinion requires no great attainments. It is ... the benefit of the Cherokees, who, you know, are uninformed."[1]

The letter was written from New Echota where the Boudinots, after a few months at High Tower, had established their home. Harriet had left the tiny mountain station regretfully. "I am much attached to this neighborhood," she wrote to Connecticut. "Almost all the people here are our relatives." But New Echota in the Conasauga valley was in familiar country. From her windows the daughter of Ben-

[1] All quotations in this chapter are from the *Vaill Mss.*

jamin Gold could see the sun rise over the Cohutta ridge reminding her, perhaps, of the days at Cornwall when she had seen the dark mass of Colt's Foot Mountain against the dawn. Spring Place, where Elias had gone to school, was only twenty miles to the north on the traders' trail. New Echota, moreover, was not an Indian town in the sense of Cowe that Bartram knew. New Echota was a tiny cluster of stores and frame houses about a council house and a court house and looked, save for the council house, like any one of a score of Georgia crossroads settlements. The village, which was the new capital of the Cherokee nation, was the result of the acceptance of white civilization in the Indian country. It symbolized the desire of the Cherokees to imitate the whites. The place swarmed with redmen when the General Council was in session.

The Worcesters lived but a stone's throw from the home of the editor of the *Phœnix*. The friendship between the two families had deepened with the passing months. Worcester and Boudinot had already embarked upon their joint labors. Harriet found in Ann Worcester a comrade to take the place of the sisters she had left in Connecticut. "You don't know what a good sister she is to me," wrote Harriet. "We are as one family. She is just your age Sister Flora."

Harriet had need of a good sister. In May, 1827, her first child was born. She named her babe Eleanor for the grandmother who had stood unmoved during those hard last days at Cornwall. Before Eleanor celebrated her third birthday, she had a sister, Mary, and a brother, William Penn. The proud father wrote that Mary had "the real Indian black eyes." No physician is mentioned in the letters. Harriet was fortunate indeed to have a woman of the stamp of Ann Worcester for neighbor and friend. Meanwhile the demands of a growing family postponed that missionary career of which Harriet had dreamed in the house of Benjamin Gold.

Wistfully Harriet sometimes thought of the Cornwall home. Distance did not decrease the strength of the ties which bound her to her own people. "I should like to visit you," she wrote, "but it is not likely we shall in several years if ever. ... I remember I once had a sister Abbey, kind and dear—whom I tenderly loved. Does she ever talk about Harriet? Or are the feelings she cherished two years ago unalterable? Those months were trying ones to me, yet I number among them some of the happiest hours of my life—when a consciousness of doing right was my only consolation. ... The place of my birth is dear to me but I love this people and with them I wish to live and die."

Elias was absorbed with his editing. Getting out a weekly newspaper practically single-handed was no small task. He made selections from the exchanges to reprint in the *Phœnix*. He prepared the weekly editorial and translated it into Cherokee. "One cannot write fast in Cherokee," he commented a little ruefully. On printing days he corrected the proofs. In addition to being editor he was business manager—a task usually involving little more than entering or discontinuing subscriptions. Occasionally, however, the manager's path was beset with thorns. Denominationalism, that plague of Protestantism, once nearly wrecked the enterprise. "You will see by the *Phœnix*," Boudinot wrote to Vaill, "that we have had a change of Printers. The former Printer Mr. Harris, who is a Methodist by religious profession has occasioned me a great deal of vexation. He has been secretly circulating falsehoods, one of which is that the *Cherokee Phœnix* is under the influence of Mr. Worcester, and has gone so far as to lodge charges in the War Department. His conduct became intolerable. Before the commencement of the year I received full authority from the principal chiefs to continue or dismiss what printers I pleased. I accordingly addressed a note to Mr. H. stating that he should be discontinued on the first day of Jan. and requested him to resign. He returned me a very insolent answer, and declared he would not deliver the office except by force, whereupon I obtained an order from the Asst. Prin. Chief by virtue of which he was dispossessed by the Marshall. He has threatened to kick me, Mr. Worcester, Mr. Ross, the Principal Chief and a host of others I believe but has not done it yet. Since his removal we get along a great deal better."

Busy as he was with the *Phœnix,* Boudinot found time to spend many hours working with Samuel Worcester. The two were collaborating in translations. Sequoyah's syllabary made it possible to open the literature of the white man to the Cherokee. Worcester and Boudinot both felt that their principal work in life was to be the making of the white man's literature and knowledge available to the Indian. Naturally these Puritans began with the translation of religious writings. A sheaf of hymns of about fifty pages was, according to Boudinot, "the first Cherokee book ever published." Even before the hymns were finished the collaborators were at work upon a Cherokee edition of Matthew's gospel.

※

Work crowded the days of Elias and Harriet Boudinot. They were true to the old Puritan admonition to be diligent. They were young. They were happy in their work because they believed they were helping the Cherokees to Christianity and civilization. They were happy in each other. Boudinot appreciated the prize he had won. Harriet wrote of her husband as one who "not only possesses, but is truly worthy of my warmest affections—my tenderest love." "I wish Br. and Sister Vaill, you could just step in, and sit . . . with us this evening. Susan, Elias' young sister sits in one corner, mending her stockings, and I in the other writing this letter — while the children are all abed and asleep. Mr. Boudinot has gone to Mr. Worcester's to pay off Mr. S. of Tennessee for our years supply of pork. . . . He works very hard. . . . His salary is also small considering his expenses—but he is willing to make some sacrifice for his country."

Neither work nor affection, however, could dispel a shadow which lay over this home. There were times when Harriet was filled with foreboding. Once she unburdened herself to her northern sister. "We know not what is before us, sometimes I fear the Cherokees will see evil days." Then one day in 1829 Harriet forgot for the moment her fears as she read the letter which announced that Benjamin and Eleanor Gold were starting for New Echota. A few weeks later a carriage which had begun its journey at Cornwall stopped before the door of Elias Boudinot.

On October 29, 1829, the aged Cornwall Puritan wrote to Flora and Herman Vaill:
"Dear & beloved Children—
We arrived here the day before yesterday in good health & good spirits—after a pretty long journey from Cornwall the 10th day of Sept'r 47 days on the road traveling every day except Sunday & two half days being two rainy & one

hole day being a very rainey day—by the great goodness of Divine Providence we have been upheld & preserved all the way in good health & free from any material harm. ... —of course it was muddy & heavy traveling the greatest part of the way—but we took it patiently & slowly all the way & enjoyed ourselves well for the most part—we were much pleased with the country & people—many very fine Towns & viliges we passed through in the states of New York, Jersey, Pennsylvany—Maryland & Virginia—then we came into Tenesee where the country appeared to be new—but the people kind & accomodating—we traveled about 400 miles in Virginia the north side of the blue ridge where we could see it for two or three hundred miles—& we often spoke of what you said in your last letter to us before we left home—Viz. that you should like to be in the bush when we were traveling along the blue Ridge & hear the Col. singing some old tune & Mother taking out her snuff box to take a pinch of snuff—we did frequently amuse ourselves by a song & pinch of snuff as we passed along that country—we were on Harrietts track where the people appeared to remember them with much interest & told us many interesting things about them. we passed the Ferry of Highvassy on thursday the 22 day of this month & set our feet on Cherokee ground & within about 100 rods arrived at the house of Mr Lewis Ross one of the Council of the Cherokee N ation & that night rained & all the next day—so that we could not think of riding—but we found ourselves in a good harbour they welcomed us in this nation—Mr Ross & his Lady were both of them at New Echota at the session of the Council with one of their children—still there were four butiful children at home — the eldest a Daughter who had been attending school at Knoxville Tenesee twelve years old a very interesting girl—Mr Ross is I believe a half breed Mrs. Ross of the old Megs family. ... Mr. Ross's House is a large & elegant white House as handsomely furnished & handsomely situated as almost any house in Litchfield County—he appears to be rich & no doubt he is so. he has around his House about 20 Negro slaves who paid good attention to us two nights—& when we offered to pay a bill they told us that Mr Ross would not take any thing for entertainment of any people who had connection in the Nation—from thence we went to the next public house about 22 miles Mr McNairs—a very grand Brick house & every accomodation around it; he is a white man & his wife a cherokee & a superior woman about half breed. ... they also made us welcome & would take nothing of us—Harriett also stayed at those two last mentioned places when she came into the country—we passed on from thence to springplace about 22 miles the old Moravian Missionary Station & put up & staid over night where they treated us kindly & would take nothing of us—next morning passed on & reached New Echota a little before sunset—about 20 miles—where we met our Dear children & friends in health & with feelings of Joy that may be better conceived than expressed—but all the way in the Nation we had no need of spending any money except at the ferries —to be short the people all appear to be perfectly friendly & many places we have seen look indeed like civilization & they tell us that many other parts which we have not yet seen are much better—we hope to be able to visit all the Missionary stations schools &c in the nation before we return—I think so far as I have seen that the land is very excelent—smoth land clear from Stone in most parts about but enough—well watered & timber is of most sorts that we have in Connecticut White oak is the greatest part & of a butiful quality—in some places it is the largest & hansomest that I ever saw in any country—but in general is of a suitable & convenient size a good proportion of hansom walnut timber & considerable good chesnut timber & whitewood almost every where interspersed with large smoth & tall pine trees & pine of all sizes

"New Echota is on a hansom spot of ground a little elevated—with a Council House & Court House in the center & two or three Merchants Stores about half a dozen hansom framed Dwelling Houses in sight which would be called respectable in Litchfield county—& very decently furnished to be in any country & all new built say within 3 or 4 years. I have been in most of the Houses & find the families very polite & agreeable pleasant & fit associates for any country. the National Council & superior Court is now here in session & I have yesterday & today attended both & seen important causes before them—have observed much order & decorum—in all their Council & Court are quite a number of learned pollished & well Qualified Gentlemen fit to appear in any place in Connecticut—I have a fine opportunity at this time & have been introduced to most of the members of the Council & the Court — am much pleased with the acqaintance I have already had—be sure some of the gentlemen are full blood Cherokees & in a rude State but easily to be seen of great natural powers of mind."

During the winter of 1829-30 Benjamin Gold had his last great adventure. He enjoyed himself to the full. In April, 1830, he wrote Herman Vaill that he would start home in June and would probably reach Connecticut five weeks later. "For my part," he added, "their good spring weather —and coffee—and as much good victuals as they give me—

keep me in pretty good plyght without any medicine whatever. ... I like the Country much and I think I should prefer the climate to that of New England. ... I traveled much ... in various parts—I rarely see, or hear of a sickly person—I think if I was a young man that I should prefer settling here to any country that I am acquainted with—but my day is pretty much past and gone and I shall have about enough to do to visit my children if my life should be prolonged as much as can be reasonably expected. ... E. Boudinot's family are all well. They send their tenderest and kindest love to you—their 3 little children grow and come on finely. William Penn among the rest is second to no boy of his age—little Mary looks out of as hansom pair of black eyes as ever was seen—Eleanor will be 3 years old the 4th of May next—appears to know as much as any girl of her age—attends Miss Sawyers school which is kept in the Court House about 30 rods from her Father's House."

Harriet wrote a postscript to her father's letter. "I feel as though the time was near when I must again say farewell to my dear parents. ... They will tell you a great deal about us when they see you. ... The children are much attached to their Grand Parents — I hardly know what I shall do with them when they are gone off. You were about to call your last baby, *Temperance,* because you dispensed with rum—what shall we do? We have had 3 without the assistance of a drop of rum—or any kind of ardent spirits—The truth is we have not bought a drop since we kept house—and I hesitate not to say (without boasting), that my husband is, and has ever been a more temperate man—than any of his brothers in law on my side. ... I assure you, this is a trying season with us as a people."

16

The White Terror

THE name William Penn had significance for Elias Boudinot. During the year 1829, when the boy was born, the editor of the *Phœnix* had followed closely in the *National Intelligencer* a series of twenty-four "Essays on the Present Crisis in the Condition of the American Indians," signed with the pseudonym, "William Penn." Their author was an old friend of Boudinot's, Jeremiah Evarts. The essays voiced a protest against the efforts of the federal authorities to persuade the eastern Cherokees to remove beyond the Mississippi. "If Christianity is the basis of the law of nations and the common law of the United States," remarked Evarts, "it surely is not out of place, though it should be unnecessary, to remind our lawgivers and judges, that one of the great maxims of Christianity, for the regulation of intercourse among men, is, that *we should do to others whatever we would desire that they, in like circumstances, should do to us.* Let the people of Georgia, and the people of the United States reflect, whether they would be willing to receive the same treatment, with which the Cherokees are threatened. Would they be content to go into exile. ...?"[1]

Perhaps, as Boudinot read Evarts' argument, he recalled

---

[1] These letters were republished under the same title in pamphlet form, Boston, 1829. Quotation from page 95.

some phrases from his own address at Philadelphia. "There is in Indian history something very melancholy, and which seems to establish a mournful precedent for the future events of the few sons of the forest, now scattered over this vast continent. We have seen everywhere the . . . aborigines melt away before the white population." But Boudinot named his boy William Penn; it was his answer to the challenge of the whites.

Clouds were gathering above the Cherokee horizon. The mutterings of race prejudice among the whites rumbled like distant thunder through the hills. Georgia was becoming restive. A considerable portion of the Cherokee territory lay within the ancient charter limits of that state. In 1802 Georgia had ceded to the United States its claims to those rich lands which now comprise the states of Alabama and Mississippi in return, among other considerations, for a pledge that the United States would free the state of Indians as soon as the removal could be effected peacefully and on reasonable terms. The Cherokees naturally felt themselves bound by no obligations arising from the compact of 1802. They were attached to their ancestral home, where every mountain had a place in tribal tradition and every valley was full of associations. For some the Immortals still lived on the peaks. The Cherokees, moreover, were making progress in civilization. Their leaders visioned a day when they would achieve a footing of equality with the whites. Other Indian nations had fought without avail to stay the advance of the frontier of civilization. The Cherokees, profiting by the mistakes of other tribes, were pursuing the more intelligent course of acquiring the culture of the conqueror.

Some of the leaders of the red mountaineers believed that the progress of the tribe toward civilization would cause the white people to look upon them with favor. In Georgia, however, Cherokee development bred apprehension. If these redskins should become truly civilized, reasoned the Georgians, they could never be dislodged and a permanent Indian population would reside in the northwest corner of the state. The situation required action before it was too late. The officials at Milledgeville began in the eighteen twenties a vigorous prodding of the lethargic central government. Through the corridors of the national capitol echoed their complaint that the United States had removed to the West only a third of the Cherokees.[2] Georgia congressmen reminded the federal government of its pledged word and its honor.

The Georgians maintained that the eastern Cherokees were a remnant of a semibarbarous tribe encumbering the territory of the state and blocking the advance of civilization. The head men of the Indians met the Georgia charge by adopting, in 1826, a written constitution patterned as far as possible after that of the United States. They replied to Georgia, in effect, that written constitutions are not the work of barbarians. Their document, moreover, opened with defiant words. "We, the Cherokee people, constituting one of the sovereign and independent nations of the earth, and having complete jurisdiction over its territory to the exclusion of the authority of every other state, do ordain this constitution." Such claims goaded the Georgians to action. The legislature, sitting in December, 1827, solemnly asserted that the title of the Cherokees to their land

---

[2] The classic account of the controversy between Georgia and the United States is Ulrich B. Phillips, *Georgia and State Rights* (Washington, Government printing office, 1902).

was temporary, that they were tenants at will, and that the state might rightfully take possession of the Indian lands by any means necessary and extend over them the laws of the commonwealth. Georgia was learning the language of might. The state notified the Washington authorities that, if the Indians were not in process of removal at the end of twelve months, Georgia would extend its laws to the Cherokee country.

The threat shook the foundations of the home of Elias and Harriet Boudinot. Boudinot fought Georgia through the columns of the *Phœnix,* addressing his reply primarily to his white subscribers in the North. "What a pernicious effect must such a document as the report of the joint committee in the legislature of Georgia, have on the interests and improvement of the Indians? Who will expect from the Cherokees a rapid progress in education, religion, agriculture, and the various arts of civilized life when resolutions are passed in a civilized and Christian legislature (whose daily sessions, we are told, commenced with a prayer to Almighty God) to wrest their country from them, and strange to tell, with the point of the bayonet, if nothing else will do? Is it in the nature of things, that the Cherokees will build good and comfortable houses and make them great farms, when they know not but their possessions will fall into the hands of strangers & invaders? How is it possible that they will establish for themselves good laws, when an attempt is made to crush their first feeble effort toward it?"[3]

More clearly than Jeremiah Evarts, Boudinot sensed the significance for the Cherokees of Georgia's action. His edu-

[3] *Cherokee Phœnix,* March 6, 1828.

cation in New England had given him perspective. He was a man of few illusions. He knew his people. They had only recently emerged from the forest and but yesterday had substituted the garb of civilization for the breech cloth. There were among them some sophisticated mixed bloods, but the mass of the people were untutored full bloods stumbling in bewilderment into a new age. The old hunting gods were dying. The legend of the redbird was being forgotten. Young men were skeptical of the shamans' magic. The Cherokees were losing hold upon the old and well-tried beliefs and ways of life. The disappearance of game was forcing upon them an exotic civilization which they did not understand. They were drifting with the tide like a ship which has lost her moorings. Eagerly they learned the characters which Sequoyah had invented. Perhaps the crippled silversmith had discovered some abracadabra that would give the Cherokee power equal to that of the engulfing white man. Elias Boudinot sensed the helplessness of a people who understood nothing of the world beyond their mountains. He knew that there was no magic formula for power. He hoped to become a leader who would guide the development of civilization among the Cherokees. He sought to replace the Little Men and the Immortals with the God of the Puritans. Sequoyah had forged the necessary tools. Samuel Worcester had the breadth of mind necessary for the transfer of the white man's literature to the Cherokee. Boudinot had become partner to Worcester and successor to Sequoyah in the task of guiding the course of Cherokee thinking. The disaster which threatened as a result of Georgia's determination would put an end to all Cherokee progress. The West, whither the tribe was being driven, was a wild country still dominated by hunters. Fierce and jealous plains tribes resented the incursions of eastern Indians into their ancient hunting grounds. Beyond the Mississippi was chaos and war.

Boudinot managed to keep his feet on the ground while holding fast to his dreams for his people. Long before the Georgia legislators bestirred themselves, he understood the menace even of the peaceful American for the Indian. When white and red met, the Indian degenerated. The chief cause was liquor. Where firewater appeared, crimes of violence multiplied, followed quickly by disease and depravity. Unlike Sequoyah, who worked alone in his cabin unmindful of the shifting Cherokee scene, Boudinot sought to combine scholarship and action. The *Phœnix* was his weapon, and through its columns he attacked intemperance. "Among us, it has been a wide spreading evil. It has cost us lives and a train of troubles. It has been an enemy to our national prosperity, industry, and intellectual improvement. Even at this day when it is generally conceded that we are the most civilized of all the Aboriginal tribes, we see this enemy of all good stalking forth in triumph, carrying desolation and misery into families and neighborhoods."[4]

Boudinot's hope was to save his people from their weaknesses as well as to lead them to civilization. He was convinced, as were his fellow Puritans, that religion is necessary to support morals. This red son of Andover believed that Christianity offered to the Indian the trail to the good and enlightened life. But he had no illusions of easy victory. He knew that even under the most favorable

[4] *Ibid.,* October 1, 1828.

conditions, the battle between good and evil in the land of the Cherokees was evenly drawn. The carrying out of the Georgia threat would mean the end of the Indian government and confusion among the people. Then must the thin battalions of righteousness be overwhelmed and the Cherokees retreat from evil to evil.

※

In 1829 the laws of Georgia were extended to the Cherokee country, replacing tribal law. A special Indian code was passed which prevented a redman from testifying in court and made two white witnesses necessary for the proving of a contract between white man and Indian. A New England humanitarian, Edward Everett, pointed out in the House of Representatives on May 19, 1830, the meaning of the new legislation. Unprincipled white men "have but to cross the Cherokee line; they have but to choose the time and the place, where the eye of no white man can rest upon them, and they may burn the dwelling, waste the farm, plunder the property, assault the person, murder the children of the Cherokee subject of Georgia, and, though hundreds of the tribe may be looking on, there is not one of them that can be permitted to bear witness against the spoiler. When I am asked, then, what the Cherokee has to fear from the law of Georgia, I answer, that, by that law, he is left at the mercy of the firebrand and dagger of every unprincipled wretch in the community."[5]

The speech was a part of a hot debate in Congress over a bill for the removal of virtually all the Indians east of the Mississippi to new homes on the western plains. Everett

[5] *Speeches on the Passage of the Bill for the Removal of the Indians, Delivered in the Congress of the United States, April and May, 1830* (Boston, Perkin & Marvin, 1830), 262.

of Massachusetts could afford to sympathize with the Indians. His Puritan ancestors had practically exterminated their redskins neighbors before the end of the eighteenth century. Everett was far removed from the zone of race contact and could apply with safety the principles of Christianity to the problem of red and white. There were many humanitarians from all over the nation who battled against the Removal Bill. But, in the end, they lost. A few days after Everett's attempt, President Andrew Jackson signed with satisfaction a measure whose purpose was to force practically all Indians in the East to remove beyond the Father of Waters.

17

Prison

THE Boudinots and Worcesters at New Echota began the year, 1831, with a day of fasting and prayer. The Cherokee government had called upon the whole nation to demonstrate in such manner their concern for the evils which the past twelve months had seen rising on every hand. During 1830 disturbing rumors came to the council house and sped on to the other settlements. Bands of roving whites were attacking isolated Indian cabins. Renegade Cherokees were joining with lawless borderers in the growing business of stealing Indian property. White intruders with no semblance of legal right were driving Indians from their houses and were appropriating the habitations for their own use. The head men of the Cherokees were frequently at New Echota holding grave discussions.

They authorized early in the year a band of Indians to strike back at the intruders. This party turned out of Indian cabins no less than seventeen families and burned the dwellings to the ground. Returning home, five of the band dawdled in a tap room and became intoxicated. In such condition they were found and attacked by more than a score of whites bent on revenge for the burnings. When the brawl ended, three Indians were prisoners and one was dead. A tense situation followed.

Samuel Worcester read with approval Elias Boudinot's

warning in the *Phœnix*. "This is a circumstance we have for a long time dreaded. ... It has been the desire of our enemies that the Cherokees may be urged to some desperate act—thus far this desire has never been realized, and we hope, notwithstanding the great injury now sustained, their wonted forbearance will be continued. If our word will have any weight with our countrymen in this very trying time, we would say, forbear, forbear—revenge not, but leave vengeance to him 'to whom vengeance belongeth.'"[1] Bitter experience had taught the Cherokees that war could end only in Indian defeat. They kept the peace.

The intruders were for the most part gold diggers, for the yellow metal had been discovered in Georgia in 1829. The gravels of the Cherokee country were proving profitable. In October, 1830, a New York paper reported that during the previous nine months more than two hundred thousand dollars worth of metal had been received in Augusta alone. The mint at Gainesville, Georgia, was stamping a hundred dollars of gold each day.[2] In the same month the Georgia legislature took drastic action to keep the wealth in the hands of citizens of the state. An armed guard was established in the Indian country to prevent the Cherokees from mining gold and to check disorder. Another act forbade the Cherokee Council to meet except for the purpose of ceding land and threatened with four years imprisonment any Indian who should presume to hold court or to act as judge. The same law provided that no white persons would be permitted to reside in the Indian country after March 1, 1831, without a license from the governor.

[1] *Cherokee Phœnix*, February 10, 1830.
[2] *Niles Register*, XXXIX, 106.

The missionaries to the Cherokees were deeply stirred by the Removal Act which Congress had passed, and by the course of Georgia. They met and publicly protested against the actions of both Georgia and the United States. They appealed to the American people to stay the hands of both governments from destroying the promising civilization of the Cherokees. Samuel and Ann Worcester quietly faced at New Echota the consequences of the missionary declaration.

In February, 1831, a daughter came to the Worcester household. Two sisters, Ann who was four and Sarah who was two, looked into the cradle of the tiny Jerusha. Their mother lay seriously ill. When the babe was scarcely more than two weeks old, the Georgia Guard appeared at the Worcester home in sufficient force to impress the Indians and took away her father. The arrest was fruitless. Worcester was found to be postmaster at New Echota and, therefore, an agent of the central government. He was soon again at the bedside of his wife.

When the April 30 number of the *Phœnix* reached him, Worcester read sadly the communication of a correspondent from that part of the Cherokee country known as Tensewaytee which portrayed the mood of some of the guard when they witnessed an outdoor baptism of Indian Christians. Boudinot published it as part of his fight against oppression. "After the solemnity of baptism was performed," said the writer, "a very mild invitation was given to the congregation to retire to the house of worship; but before the congregation had retired from the water the following . . . scene took place among the Geo. Guard. Three of their number pretended that they were so powerfully moved upon by the Spirit, that they mounted their fine horses, returned to the place of baptism, telling the people to get out of their way or else they would ride over them, for they were determined to baptize their horses in the same place. They rode into the water mocking religion and repeating the sacred words of our blessed Saviour."

Samuel Worcester did not fail to recognize the significance of a message he received from Washington a few weeks later dismissing him from his postmastership. On July 7, 1831, he was again a prisoner. Ann Worcester, alone, struggled to regain her health. In August she covered the face of her dead baby. A month later her husband was sentenced to four years at hard labor in the state penitentiary. At any time he could have avoided imprisonment by taking an oath of allegiance to Georgia and submitting to her laws. After his conviction, such an act would at any time have opened the doors of his prison. Such action, he considered, would be a betrayal of the Cherokees. He remained defiant. Defiant also was Ann Worcester when, at the end of the first year of her husband's imprisonment she took her two remaining daughters to visit their father. The missionaries had carried their case to the Supreme Court of the United States.

On the third of March, 1832, John Marshall handed down the decision which declared the Georgia enactment unconstitutional and which gave Samuel Worcester his place in American history. Immediately the clerk of the court prepared a mandate ordering "that all proceedings of the said indictment do forever surcease, and that the said Samuel A. Worcester be, and hereby is, henceforth, dismissed therefrom, and that he go thereof, quit without day."

March, 1832, found Elias Boudinot and his cousin and former Cornwall schoolmate, John Ridge, in Boston. They were completing a speaking tour of the North in which they were trying to mobilize support for the Cherokees. On March 7, Boudinot sent his brother Stand Watie, who was editing the *Phœnix* in his absence, a description of the scene in the Mission Rooms of the A.B.C.F.M. when the news of the Marshall decision reached them. "Expectation has for the last few days been upon tip-toe—fears and hopes alternately took possession of our minds until two or three hours ago Mr. John Tappan came in to see us. . . . He then told us the true story of the case, and produced a paper which contained an account, and tried to read to us, but he was so agitated with joy that he could hardly proceed. . . . Soon after Dr. [Lyman] Beecher came—I asked him whether he had heard the news from Washington. He said, 'No, what is it?' I told him the Supreme C. had decided in favor of the Missionaries. He jumped up, clapped his hands, took hold of my hand and said, 'God be praised,' and ran right out to tell his daughter and his family. . . . It is a great triumph on the part of the Cherokees. . . . The question is forever settled as to who is right and who is wrong. . . . Your letter found me very feeble. Brother Franklin Gold has come all the way from New Hampshire to see me. . . . Tell Harriet I have written her almost every week—and generally long letters. . . ."[8]

During the summer of 1832, however, Elias Boudinot learned the full strength of race hatred. Georgia quietly ignored the mandate of the Supreme Court. President

---

[8] Edward E. Dale and Gaston Litton, *Cherokee Cavaliers* (Norman, University of Oklahoma Press, 1939), 4-7.

Andrew Jackson took no steps to support the chief tribunal of the United States. The decision became John Marshall's most famous scrap of paper.

In January, 1833, Worcester was released. As a condition of the governor's pardon he had promised to depart from Georgia's area. He understood clearly that not only he but the Cherokees had lost the battle. He knew that they must give up their ancient homeland and build their habitations beyond the Mississippi. He immediately began to make plans to go to what was then called Arkansas. In the spring of 1835 Worcester and his family said their last good-byes to the mountains of the Cherokees.

Boudinot returned from Boston to New Echota in the summer of 1832. He also did not fail to understand the significance for the Cherokees of Georgia's successful nullification. In September he resigned as editor of the *Phœnix*, under pressure from the tribal government.

18

John Ross

ELIAS BOUDINOT resigned from the *Phœnix* because his editorial policy interfered with the purposes of the most powerful man in the Cherokee Nation.[1] John Ross, Principal Chief, was not embarrassed by academic scruples regarding the freedom of the press. To Boudinot it seemed that the act of Georgia and the United States compelled the Indians to consider the question of removal. The columns of the *Phœnix* seemed to him a proper place to carry on a public discussion. Ross forbade the editor to print a word in favor of removal. The will of the Principal Chief prevailed. In September, 1832, Elijah Hicks, who lived at New Echota and who was brother-in-law to Ross, took the vacant chair at the editorial desk. In his first number the new editor wrote concerning his predecessor and old neighbor that the loss of Boudinot from the paper was "but a drop from the bucket."

John Ross was forty-two in the autumn in which he disposed of Elias Boudinot.[2] He lived in a fine house near the head of the Coosa River where he combined the rôles of

---

[1] For a detailed and documented account of the circumstances surrounding Boudinot's resignation, see E. Boudinot, *Letters and Other Papers Relating to Cherokee Affairs* (Athens, Ga., printed at the office of the "Southern Banner," 1837), 1-18. See also *Ex. Doc.* 292, No. 286, 24 Cong., 1 sess., 62.

[2] An excellent, though somewhat laudatory, biography is that of Rachel Caroline Eaton, *John Ross and the Cherokee Indians* (Muskogee, Oklahoma, The Star Printery, Inc., 1921). This chapter is under heavy debt to the Eaton account.

merchant and planter. Negro slaves waited upon him and upon Quata, his full-blood Cherokee wife. He was rich, even according to the standards of the whites. He had the reserved and dignified manner of the Indian and the urbanity of the white planter. His polish and his perfect English never failed to impress the Washington politicians with whom he frequently had dealings.

Ross's blue eyes and brown hair proclaimed him no pure blood. The Cherokee strain, in fact, accounted for only one-eighth of his heritage. Ross was a Scotchman with a dash of Cherokee blood. His father, Daniel Ross, and his maternal grandfather, John McDonald, had spent practically their whole adult lives as traders among the Cherokees.

As a boy John Ross was one of the swarm of Indian children who played about the cabins of the town where his successful father carried on his business. One of Ross's earliest and most painful recollections related to a day during the celebration by the Cherokees of the Green Corn Dance when his proud mother decked him out in a white boy's suit and his playfellows jeered him out of their company. On the next day John was again an Indian. But Daniel Ross had a conscience. Though he had cast his lot with the Cherokees, he was unwilling to see his sons grow up to be ignorant hunters and his daughters to be mere planters of corn and dressers of skins. He imported a schoolmaster and on his own property opened the first school in the Cherokee Nation. In course of time John Ross and his brother, Lewis, were enrolled at a frontier institution, hopefully called an academy, at Kingston, Tennessee.

When his schooling was done, young John Ross, with two partners, Lewis and John Meigs, son of the famous Indian agent, Return Jonathan Meigs, opened a store where the shadow of Lookout Mountain falls across the bank of the lazy Tennessee. The existence of the present Chattanooga near the site of Ross's Landing suggests the foresight of the trio. The trading establishment prospered; but the excitement of barter and the thrill of profits failed to satisfy the restless spirit of young John Ross.

For all his white blood and his white boy's education, Ross of necessity looked upon himself as an Indian. His eighth of Indian blood fixed his status among the whites. Among them no "breed" could hope for a career. His marriage to Quata was his formal acceptance of the fate which had cast his lot among the Cherokees. As he left school, these Indians were being slowly forced to substitute farming for hunting. Many of his childhood playfellows, grown to manhood, were cultivating tiny clearings in the valley bottoms. They had no ambition except to get a little food and some whiskey. John Ross set out to show his contempt for the dull Indian and the stupid white borderer by winning wealth and fame.

He made his political start by opposing Tecumseh when the great Shawnee tried to bring the southern Indians into his confederacy. In 1814 Ross was one of the more prominent among the Cherokee warriors who helped Andrew Jackson defeat the Creeks at Horseshoe Bend. Americans were still celebrating Old Hickory's victory over Pakenham at New Orleans when the Cherokees found themselves facing Andrew Jackson himself, commissioned by the United States to negotiate for their removal beyond the Mississippi. The mixed bloods, who were already beginning to get political power into their hands, saw that danger lurked in the loose governmental organization of the tribe. The chiefs of the different towns managed their separate affairs much as they pleased, with the result that united tribal action was virtually impossible. Unless such decentralization were ended, approachable chiefs were sure to sell their lands and the Cherokees to find themselves trekking westward. The crisis presented by the Jackson negotiations enabled the mixed bloods to set up a small governing body known as the National Committee, which derived its power from the General Council (meeting of all the members) of the tribe. The sons of James Vann were prominent in effecting the change, as was also Charles Hicks, who had not long before knelt at the feet of Brother John Gambold and received the sacrament of the Lord's Supper. In 1819 John Ross became president of the National Committee. One of the older men who helped to speed his political advancement was Major Ridge, a liberal-minded fullblood, a man of some property and an uncle of Elias Boudinot. Ridge was one of the most sagacious and most influential men in the Nation.

※

Cherokee land was owned in common by the tribe. The tribesman might select for his plantation or his store any spot he chose as long as someone had not preceded him. Indian law gave him title to his improvements. Much of the mountainous Cherokee country was unoccupied and undeveloped, for the area was much too large for the fifteen thousand Indians to utilize in agriculture. Under such circumstances and under such a land system it is not difficult to understand how the small group of mixed bloods who by the 1820's controlled the tribal government were at the same time possessed of the principal ferries, the most advantageous trading sites, and the best plantation land of the

Nation. But Ross aspired to political leadership more than to wealth.

In 1826 the mixed bloods, by means of the constitution already mentioned, reorganized the government which the representatives of Georgia at Washington had called barbarian. The new arrangement consisted of a bicameral legislature and a single executive, the principal chief. To this office Ross was elevated, and in it he became virtually dictator. His dictatorship, like those a century later in Europe, was the fruit of insecurity. The threatened Cherokees sought safety in the leadership of a single champion.

Ross became a leader of mixed bloods because no one of them could match him in dealing with the representatives of the United States. They were bound to him because removal beyond the Mississippi meant the end of their wealth and special opportunities. He was idealized by the mass of ignorant Indians who were groping toward civilization. In those days when the very foundations of their lives seemed to be dissolving, the untutored Cherokees clung to the hills, terrified lest the white man should deprive them of that homeland which was their only contact with the past. Where was the Indian who did not remember that dramatic day in 1823 when John Ross, amid impressive silence, had risen in the Council and had exposed the attempt of two United States commissioners to bribe him into favoring a treaty of sale for the lands of the Cherokees? Since then Ross had been fighting to save their lands for them. He was rich. He knew more than any of the medicine men of old. Their magic had failed. Ross said he would not permit the white man to drive them from their mountains. He knew whereof he spoke. He was greater than all the medicine men. His magic would succeed.

But the power of John Ross did not spring entirely from his artistry in leadership. He controlled the annuities which, as a price of former land cessions, the United States paid to the tribal government. Much of this income went to pay salaries to the ruling group—including the editor of the *Cherokee Phœnix*. The people were not taxed to support their government. Possession of the money bags, however, did not complete the edifice of Ross's power. In the same year in which the new constitution was being framed the mixed bloods had issued a formal warning: "Resolved by the National Committee and Council, That any person or persons, whatever, who shall be found guilty of forming unlawful meetings, to encourage rebellion against the laws and government of the Cherokee Nation, shall receive one hundred stripes on the bare back."[3] Two years later, October 26, 1829, the Cherokee government revived and put in writing an old law that any individual who sold land without the special permission of the tribal authorities should be punished by death.

The acts of Georgia and of the United States left John Ross unmoved. He continued to fight for the Cherokee homeland. His own stake in the country was large. He was at the same time obeying the mandate of his people. If the tribe should migrate and join with the western Cherokees, what would become of that efficient political structure which had been built up in the southern mountains—what would become of the power of the principal chief? In the face of almost certain defeat Ross was determined to continue to fight.

In 1832 Major Ridge, John Ridge, and Elias Boudinot

[3] *Ex. Doc.* 292, No. 286, 24 Cong., 1 sess., 76.

at the risk of their lives defied the Principal Chief. Like Samuel Worcester they were convinced that the Cherokee cause was hopeless. The time for retreat had come. Continued opposition to Georgia and the United States could only make worse the disaster which had befallen their people.

19

Red Clay

OCTOBER, 1835, found the Cherokees filling the trails which led to Red Clay, located where the boundary between Tennessee and Georgia crosses what is now Mills Creek.[1] In this town, hidden in the hill country west of the Conasauga valley, a National Council was to be held. Because of the Georgia laws New Echota had for some time been abandoned as the tribal capital. At Red Clay in Tennessee the hated Georgia Guards had no jurisdiction.

An unusual number of Indians journeyed to Red Clay, for rumor said that important decisions would be made. On the trail and in camp the talk was of hardship and suffering. Old friends of the Moravians noted that the missionaries were no longer at Spring Place. On the afternoon of January 1, 1833, twenty people in wagons and carts had driven up to that station and had demanded immediate possession. They said that they had drawn this prize in the lottery by which Georgia was distributing to its citizens the lands which the Cherokees still continued to occupy. That night, for the first time in thirty years, Spring Place heard no sound of hymns. "To abandon this time-honored spot," wrote Brother Clauder mournfully, "where the first

---

[1] The story of the Red Clay negotiations is based on the voluminous correspondence in the Indian Office Manuscript Records and on the mass of documents published in *Ex. Doc. 292*, No. 286, 24 Cong., 1 sess.

convert from the Cherokee tribe was baptized in 1810; where first the feet of them that brought glad tidings of great joy rested in their travel to this tribe of Indians and where so many prayers and tears had been offered to God and so many tokens of his goodness witnessed—this was a consideration far more painful than any amount of unrighteousness inflicted upon us by the miserable wretches around us. But the Lord gave us enlargement."[2]

Since the evacuation of Spring Place the Georgians had crowded into the Indian country. Scores of Cherokee families had been thrust from their cabins, and their crops and cattle appropriated. Many of the men and women who trudged to Red Clay were homeless and hungry. They knew not where to turn nor what to do. Their one hope was John Ross, their man of magic who had talked even with the president of the United States. They saw him at the council ground always dignified, always polite, and always busy with their poor affairs. Behind his calm exterior they did not know that Ross was seeking anxiously for a solution for the most difficult problem of his political career.

Elias Boudinot journeyed with the rest to Red Clay. The storm which had raged within him had subsided, and now he too was calm and self-possessed. His decision had been made. To the southwest across the valley of the Conasauga he could see, as he traveled, the distant heights of Cohutta Mountain. How many times had Harriet and he watched from their home at New Echota the play of light on these wooded uplands! Within sight of this mass of rock he had been born, had gone to school at Spring Place, and, upon his

[2] Schwarze, *History of the Moravian Missions,* 201 f.

return from New England, had worked for the betterment of his people. He loved the land of his fathers, but he had made up his mind to leave it.

Underneath the disciplined intelligence of Boudinot was the emotion of the Indian. Among the primitive Cherokees this had found expression in haunting chants and wild dances and in a religion which gave spiritual meaning to the aspects of nature about them. Boudinot's training had made the chant and the dance impossible for him. His feelings found vent in an almost fierce tribal loyalty—a loyalty to a dream of a civilized Cherokee nation.

Fate had dealt strangely with Elias Boudinot. To the white race this Indian owed almost everything worth-while in life—enlightenment, faith, friends, wife. Its blood ran in the veins of his children. Yet now he saw this same race ruthlessly crushing his people, by violence despoiling them of their homes, with liquor robbing them of their character. The white man was destroying the first fruits of their efforts to lift themselves to civilization. The enlightenment which the white race had given to Boudinot enabled him to appreciate, as his people could not, the fullness of the disaster which that same race was forcing upon them. The loss of the Cherokee homeland seemed to him small when compared with that loss of character and culture which must result in degeneracy and degradation. There was no time to lose. The forces of disintegration were on every hand. Boudinot was hurrying to Red Clay to say to his people: "You must not remain longer in contact with the whites. Your safety lies in isolation. Fly—fly for your lives."

As he traveled, he smiled, perhaps, at the remembrance of events which had transpired in Washington during the previous winter. When month after month had gone by and John Ross had refused to negotiate a treaty of removal Elias Boudinot and John Ridge had gone to the national capital to force the hand of the Principal Chief. They believed that the tribesmen would vote for the removal if the question were put fairly before them and every aspect of the situation discussed. The Ross policy had been to prevent discussion at all costs. With Lewis Cass, Secretary of War, Ridge and Boudinot had begun the formulation of a treaty. For once Ross had lost his composure; his dictatorship was threatened. Thoroughly frightened he had called upon Secretary Cass and had offered to negotiate a treaty of sale and removal. He demanded twenty million dollars for the Cherokee lands. Cass had told him the sum was impossible. Ross had sensed that his status in the eyes of the government was uncertain. Under the constitution of 1826 he had been elected to office in 1828 for two years. No further elections had been held under the plea that they were impossible as a result of Georgia's actions. Might not the government refuse to admit that he had any legal authority to negotiate a treaty? With such thoughts in his mind, perhaps, Ross had offered to sell the Cherokee country at a price to be fixed by the United States Senate. That body set the figure at five million dollars. When Ross protested, Cass resumed negotiations with Ridge and Boudinot. Before he left Washington in the spring of 1835 the discomfited Principal Chief had pledged himself to urge the Cherokees to ratify the treaty. His opportunity to carry out his word came at the Red Clay council in October.

※

John Ross began his preparations for the annual Council with a friendly letter to Major Ridge in which he suggested that the Cherokees should make an end of factional strife and should present a united front to the two commissioners of the United States who were coming to Red Clay to complete the negotiations which had been started in Washington. The treaty party, headed by Boudinot and the Ridges, believed that, at last, John Ross was snared. They cheerfully accepted his proffer of friendship and the hatchet was buried. A committee of twenty, which included the three chiefs of the faction favoring a treaty, was created by the Cherokees to treat with the commissioners from Washington.

These gentlemen made a curious pair. The lesser of the two, Major B. F. Curry, was an insolent individual who was enjoying to the full his momentary responsibility. He took no pains to conceal his purpose to eject the Cherokees from the white man's country at the earliest possible moment. With satisfaction he said to Ross that Tennessee was soon to pass laws regarding the Indians akin to those of Georgia.

Curry's chief was the Reverend John F. Schermerhorn, of Utica, New York. The odor of the meeting house clung to him and his conversation was full of pious sentiments. His appointment was doubtless considered a master stroke by the War Department. Christianity was rapidly spreading among the Cherokees as the prestige of the old hunting deities faded. The Indian Christian had learned from the lives of such men as John Gambold and Samuel Worcester to respect the minister of the Gospel. Schermerhorn was the sanctimonious glove concealing the fist of that uncompromising hater of Indians, Andrew Jackson, President of the United States. Jackson, irritated at the long delay and the futile maneuverings of his subordinates, was determined that the Cherokees should be removed without more ado. Schermerhorn's task was to present to the people of the tribe the treaty which had been negotiated in Washington during the previous winter. Ross's pledge to support the instrument seemed to make its acceptance practically sure. John Ross, between Boudinot on the one hand and Old Hickory on the other, was as fairly caught as the Cherokee rabbit had once been by the wolves.

But, if Elias Boudinot and John Ridge thought they had snared their rabbit, they had forgotten the ending of the old tribal tale. It seems not to have occurred to Boudinot or the Ridges that the reconciliation which Ross had engineered with them had landed them safely in the hunting bag of the Principal Chief. Day after day the Council wore on. The mass of routine business was augmented by the large number of cases of individual distress which had to be considered. Day after day Schermerhorn meditated his speech to the tribe and wondered when he would be called upon to give it. Some of the people grew restive. In spite of the fact that four or five advocates of removal had been assassinated during the summer, there were some tribesmen courageous enough to start a movement to demand that the Committee of Twenty enter into a treaty. The man of magic checked the proposal with a statement that the Committee had the matter in hand.

Meanwhile Ross had politely asked Schermerhorn for evidence that he was authorized to negotiate a treaty. The commissioner produced an informal letter from Lewis Cass. Ross blandly remarked that it was an interesting note and that he would like now to see the formal commission. No such document existed. Then the Principal Chief informed the clergyman that, since there were no commissioners of the United States at Red Clay, the Committee of Twenty was under the necessity of going to Washington.

Then Ross appeared before the National Council. The session was about to end. The assembly of Indians looked expectantly at the Principal Chief as he rose to speak. He made no address. He merely asked if the Cherokees were willing to sell their homeland for five million dollars. The answer boomed back: "No!" He then asked if they were willing to have the Committee of Twenty continue to deal with the United States. "Yes," shouted the crowd. Then the National Council terminated. Almost at once the Indians began scattering to their homes.

The dazed Schermerhorn reported the collapse of the negotiations to his chief, Lewis Cass. He added, perhaps for the encouragement of Old Hickory: "But the Lord is able to overrule all things for good."[3]

[3] Schermerhorn to Commissioner of Indian Affairs, October 27, 1835, in the manuscript files of the Indian Bureau.

20

A Question of Ethics

ELIAS BOUDINOT and John Ridge were discomfited by the unexpected triumph of John Ross. Perhaps they reflected that the amateur challenges the seasoned politician at his peril. They were determined, however, to continue to press for a treaty that would remove the suffering Cherokees to a safe distance from the moral devastation wrought by the white intruders. Swallowing their pride, Ridge and Boudinot decided to follow Ross to Washington as members of the Committee of Twenty and to resume the old struggle.[1] They called on the frustrated Schermerhorn and inquired about his plans. He reminded them that he had instructions to call a special council of the Cherokees upon his own authority in the event of the breakdown of the Red Clay negotiations. The treaty men, chastened by the recent demonstration of Ross's political power, argued against the course and urged the commissioner to resume the negotiations in the national capital. Schermerhorn angrily informed the two Indians that he would issue the call for the council at once.

On November 3, Schermerhorn distributed a notice throughout the Cherokee Nation. "To the Chiefs, Headmen, and People of the Cherokee Nations of Indians. Friends. The United States Commissioners by the direction

---

[1] Chapter XX is based on the same collections of documents used in Chapter XIX.

of the President of the U. States do hereby notify you to meet them in a General Council of the Nation; after the manner of your old usages and customs, on the third Monday of December next . . . then and there to deliberate and determine and settle by a treaty all the difficulties between the Cherokees and the United States." The reference to "old usages and customs" meant to return to the almost complete democracy which had prevailed before the mixed bloods began to centralize the government of the Indians. "The delegation or committee, whom you appointed at your Council at Red Clay," the notice continued, "and whom you expected would settle all your difficulties there with the commissioners there present, would not hear him nor listen to the liberal propositions of the Government for a moment; but were determined before hand to go to Washington; and we know not for what unless they were afraid to let you [know] what they meant to do; or else to try to get your money into their own hands which they knew the commissioners would not give them. . . ."

After reading the notice, Ridge and Boudinot conferred with the Principal Chief. They reminded him of Schermerhorn's warning that no official at Washington would treat with the delegation. Would it not be the part of wisdom, they asked, to resume negotiations in December at New Echota? Ross was adamant; he would go to Washington. By the second of the two notes of the General Council he now had the specific authority to negotiate a treaty, which he had lacked the year before. Boudinot discovered also that Ross intended to treat as binding the vote of the Cherokees against accepting five millions dollars for their land. The former editor of the *Phoenix* was convinced that the United States would negotiate on no other terms. He suspected that the Principal Chief merely intended to continue the impasse. Boudinot and Ridge, nevertheless, determined to accompany the other members of the Committee to Washington.

On the night of November 10, as the Cherokee officials were preparing for the journey north, Georgia suddenly intervened. The Guards of that state invaded Tennessee to arrest John Ross and a guest of his, John Howard Payne. The two were clapped into jail, Payne on the ground that he was a white man residing without license in the Indian country. The playwright at the moment was promoting a new magazine "in which English and American writers may meet upon equal ground." His trip to the Cherokee Country came at a time when the attempts of the United States to remove those Indians was receiving much publicity in the American press. Through some articles of his own he was hoping to make the Cherokee's troubles aid in the launching of his new journal. Ross, an adept at the art of turning defeat into victory, saw in his new friend an ally for himself and the Cherokees. After several days the two prisoners were released without explanation. The enraged author of "Home Sweet Home" immediately issued a statement regarding the wrongs of the Cherokees. As this dispatch traveled to newspaper offices all over the country, it was accompanied by an appeal from the Cherokee people and addressed to all Americans. The appeal was written by Ross, though some persons at the time were sure they could also detect suggestions of the style of Payne in the composition.

John Ridge was already on his way to Washington when he read, with rising anger, the Payne statement and its companion piece. The Cherokees were made to say that they did not wish to give up their homeland and go west, that they would prefer to remain in the east as citizens of Alabama, Tennessee, and Georgia, and that a small group among the Indians had been seduced by the United States into spreading falsehoods about the Cherokee officers and into favoring migration. Ridge was enraged at the effrontery which would make the Indians express a desire to become citizens of eastern states when such a contingency had never been discussed by them in tribal council. He was unwilling, moreover, to ignore the personal attack upon himself, his father, and Elias Boudinot. He resigned from the Committee. Boudinot also resigned, with the added reason that there was sickness in his home.

Ross, who had now launched the publicity which would be most useful to him at Washington, was anxious not to break with the treaty party. He parleyed, and Ridge finally consented to go to Washington in the forlorn hope of making a treaty which would put an end to the rapid demoralization of the Indians by the whites. He did not give up hope until Ross had failed.

At Washington the Principal Chief hopefully approached the Secretary of War and promptly discovered the consequences of opposing the will of Andrew Jackson. With emotions which he did not disclose he read a note from the Commissioner of Indian Affairs: "The delegation of the Cherokee nation, of which some of you are members, and which visited this city last winter, was emphatically assured during the last session of Congress, and that assurance was officially repeated in the course of the following autumn, that no delegation would be received here to make a treaty; and in defiance of that notification, you have come on and presented yourselves for that purpose. How could you, under such circumstances, imagine that you would be received by the Department as the duly constituted representatives of the Cherokee people? It is not easy to account for that strange error of opinion, unless it arose from the courtesy with which you were treated, when you called upon the President and the Secretary of War." The Jackson Administration was confident that the Council which Schermerhorn had called to meet at New Echota would ratify the treaty.

On December 21, 1835, the Reverend John Schermerhorn was at New Echota, hopefully waiting for the Cherokees to assemble. He had issued a warning that those members of the tribe who remained absent would be counted as favoring removal. Blankets and food were offered as additional inducements for those who came. For the past few days individuals and families had straggled in, some attracted by the government stores, others prompted by a genuine conviction that the time had come for surrender and the making of a removal treaty. On the day appointed for the opening of the Council Schermerhorn from the platform looked out over an assembly which at best could boast of being no more than a handful of the numerous Cherokee Nation. It was patent to the commissioner that the Principal Chief had again defeated him. The followers of Ross, an overwhelming majority of the Nation, had refused to come to New Echota. Andrew Jackson might dominate Washington, but John Ross still ruled in the mountains. He had elevated passive resistance to a fine art.

In his best pulpit manner Schermerhorn explained to the Cherokees before him the blessings which the United

States proposed to bestow upon them by compelling them to give up their old homes and to remove to a distant country. Elias Boudinot, listening, found himself facing the most important crisis of his life.

※

Boudinot pondered a difficult problem. His travels beyond the southern mountains and his white man's education had given him an enlarged outlook. He could see deterioration among the Cherokees resulting from contact with the aggressive whites. He saw that even the Cherokee aptitude for assimilating white civilization would not save them when their property was at the mercy of the intruder and the ancient social controls within the nation were nullified by the actions of Georgia. Tribesmen who had never been away from the mountains could not conceive of starting life afresh in a distant and strange country. Perhaps some of them believed that the Immortals who dwelt on the bare mountain peaks would still save them. For Boudinot the Immortals were part of tribal folklore belonging to an age that could never return. Boudinot put his faith in the white man's god. The essence of the religion he had learned, from Sister Gambold at Spring Place, from Herman Daggett at Cornwall, and from his teachers at Andover, was a sense of duty. It commanded him to strive against evil and to work for righteousness. His reason told him that, if the Cherokees would save their integrity, they must flee the white man as they would the pestilence. Boudinot's tribal loyalty supported his Puritan sense of duty. A handful of mountain Indians could not long defy both Georgia and the United States. In the isolation of a new frontier they might reëstablish the social discipline which would turn retrogression into progress.

At Cornwall, Boudinot had learned the Puritan answer to that old question: Am I my brother's keeper? The Puritan declared that no man can live wholly unto himself. Boudinot's enlarged vision placed upon him a responsibility he could not shirk. As missionary and editor he had devoted his life to bringing enlightenment and Christianity to his people. He was a full blood in whose heart the flame of a fierce nationalism burned. Events had created for Elias Boudinot a cruel dilemma. He could not be true to his sense of obligation to his God and to his people if he did not attempt some overt action, when opportunity offered, to force them to retreat as the only means of avoiding impending calamity. Loyalty drove him to what his people called disloyalty.

Could Boudinot and the Ridges make a treaty in the name of a people who by staying away from New Echota had declared that they would not consent to Andrew Jackson's proposals? The three did not hesitate. In the face of the tribal law decreeing death to any member who signed away land these men with a few followers put their names to an instrument which was a slightly revamped version of the treaty drawn up at Washington during the previous winter. Boudinot refused to give up his dream of a Cherokee civilization equal in intellectual and moral achievement to that of the white man. As he faced the contempt and anger of old friends and neighbors his consolation was the belief that one day his people would say that he had seen the realities more clearly than the majority and that he had done right.

In the months which followed the signing, as Elias Boudinot looked about him in the mountains, he became aware that his action had strengthened the power of the Principal

Chief. Only a few Indians left for the West. The mass of the people remained quietly in their old homes. They were still resisting passively when the aged Jackson stepped down from the presidency, leaving Martin Van Buren as his successor. The Cherokees could not believe that the United States would enforce against them a treaty which they had never made and against which they had never ceased to protest.

21

Harriet

IF the storm caused by the Georgia aggressions grew menacing outside the home of Harriet Boudinot, peace obtained within the habitation. Harriet was a mystic. Her migration from New England to the Indian country had been little more than an external change for her; the fundamentals of her life, her faith and her moral code, remained unchanged. As she grew in years, her religion deepened. Her dependence upon a Power greater than any known to earth gave her poise and serenity.

There were times when her mind ran back to those strange last months at Cornwall. "I think it is this day 6 years since I received the hand of Mr. Boudinot," she wrote to Flora in 1832, "and gave my own in the covenant of marriage. I now look back to that day with pleasure, and with gratitude. Yes I am thankful. I remember the trials I had to encounter—the thorny path I had to tread, the bitter cup I had to drink—but a consciousness of doing right—a kind and affectionate devoted husband, together with many other blessings have made amends for all. Truly I have, ere this, entered upon the 'sober realities of married life,—and if tears have been shed for me on that account—I can now pronounce them useless tears."[1]

Harriet was following in the footsteps of Eleanor Gold.

[1] *Vaill Mss.*

Her destiny was to bring forth children and to work and care for them through endless days. Only for brief intervals was the cradle empty. In less than nine years she bore three sons and three daughters.

Busy as she was with a growing family, the granddaughter of Hezekiah Gold made an impression on the Indian community. The Cherokees respected and loved this white woman who had cast her lot with them. Her fame ran beyond the limits of New Echota. "Even the people of Georgia," wrote Elias Boudinot in 1836, "not infrequently carried away by overwrought passions and prejudices against our race, such as personally knew her, or had heard of her from report, have testified to her worth and unsullied character. Some who best knew her have said, 'they never knew such a woman.'"[2]

In the spring of 1835 Harriet said good-bye to her close friend, Ann Worcester, who was leaving for the country beyond the Mississippi. It was a cheerful parting, for the two looked forward to being reunited within a year. The intellectual partnership between Elias Boudinot and Samuel Worcester was to be continued in the West. But in the autumn Harriet became ill. By winter the long threatening storm was beating against her house, but from an unexpected quarter. After the December treaty Elias Boudinot and a handful of others stood before their people as traitors. In what was said to be a fraudulent instrument they had signed away the ancient homeland of the Cherokees.

For the second time Harriet faced the open hostility of the community in which she lived and to which she was deeply attached. But Harriet no longer had her youth. In

[2] *Ibid.*

May her seventh babe, a son, was born dead. Her strength failed. The Raven Mockers of the Cherokees flew stealthily down the valley of the Conasauga and alighted above the door of Elias Boudinot.

"She suffered extreme bodily pain throughout her whole sickness," Elias wrote in August, 1836, "and it had considerable effect upon her mind. She complained of darkness in the fore part of it—but towards the latter, she said her darkness was removed, that there was a clear sky between her and her Redeemer. The morning before she died, after the most distressing night she had had, she called us to her bed. Upon my enquiring how she did, she replied that she was in great distress, (meaning her bodily distress)—'I hope,' she said, 'this is the last night I shall spend in this world, then how sweet will be the Conqueror's song.' Are your doubts removed? 'Yes.' Are you happy notwithstanding all your bodily pain and affliction? 'I am happy.' "[3]

[3] *Ibid.*

22

A Humble Individual

JOHN ROSS never displayed his talents to better advantage than in his long and bitter struggle against the Treaty of New Echota. Sympathy for the underdog is a persisting American trait, and Ross played skillfully upon this string. "In truth our cause is your own," he said to the whites. "It is the cause of liberty and justice." Many Americans were aroused by the manifest truth of this contention. "We have learned your religion also," added the Principal Chief. "We have read your sacred books. Hundreds of our people have embraced their doctrines, practiced the virtues they teach, cherished the hopes they awaken, and rejoiced in the consolations they afford." Such words could not be ignored by the thousands of conscientious American churchgoers. "We are indeed an afflicted people!" continued Ross. "Our spirits are subdued! Despair has well nigh seized upon our energies! But we speak to the representatives of a Christian country; the friends of justice; the patrons of the oppressed. ... Spare our people! Spare the wreck of our prosperity."[1]

The sentiments were the same as those which Elias Boudinot had constantly expressed in public print and private letter in the first years of the decade. Hard reality, however,

---

[1] From a memorial of the Cherokees to the Senate and House of Representatives. Printed in *Letters from John Ross ... to a Gentleman of Philadelphia, 1837* (Philadelphia, 1838), 23.

had driven him to the conviction that the whites could not save the Indians—that the Cherokees must save themselves by flight. He disliked the Ross publicity because it tended to create among the uninformed the impression that a Cherokee idyl was being ended. Boudinot knew there had never been a Cherokee idyl. The deteriorating influence of contact with the whites made an Indian arcadia impossible. He finally became exasperated at the continued indirect slurs upon the two Ridges and himself. While Harriet lived, Boudinot did not reply to his adversaries but, when the grave claimed her, he advanced to the attack. In 1837 he addressed a pamphlet to the same American public which was listening to the appeals of Ross. It demonstrates how completely Boudinot's decision to sign the treaty of 1835 was made within the framework of Puritan ethics.

"You have indirectly charged me with hypocrisy, servility, duplicity, and the like, which, if true, must for ever degrade me in the eye of a virtuous community," said Boudinot to Ross. ". . . In this controversy I am well aware of the disadvantages under which I labor. I am but an humble individual. . . . You, on the other hand, have presented yourself, as the 'Principal Chief'. . . .

"And how is it possible that I can receive any extra pecuniary advantage under the present treaty? — To be sure I might have had the same opportunities, with some of my countrymen, to speculate upon the ignorance and credulity of our citizens—I could as easily have taken advantage of their weakness, and ingratiated myself into their good favor, by pretending to be a land lover, and deluding them with hopes and expectations, which I myself did not believe would be realized, and under that deep delusion into which our people have been thrown, I could have purchased their possessions and claims for a trifle, and thus have enriched myself upon the spoils of my countrymen. But I have detested that vile speculation. . . .

"It is with sincere regret that I notice you say little or nothing about the moral condition of this people, as affected by present circumstances. I have searched in vain, in all your late communications, for some indication of your sensibility upon this point. You seem to be absorbed altogether in the pecuniary aspect of this nation's affairs—hence your extravagant demands for the lands we are compelled to relinquish — your ideas of the value of the gold mines, (which, if they had been peaceably possessed by the Cherokees, would have ruined them as soon as the operation of the State laws have done) of the value of our marble quarries, our mountains and forests. Indeed, you seem to have forgotten that your people are a community of moral beings, capable of an elevation to an equal standing with the most civilized and virtuous, or a deterioration to the level of the most degraded of our race. Upon what principle then, could you have made the assertion, that you are reported to have made, 'that the Cherokees had not suffered one half what their country was worth,' but upon the principle of valuing your nation in dollars and cents? If you mean simply the physical sufferings of this people, your assertions may be listened to with some patience; but can it be possible, that you, who have claimed to be their leader and guardian, have forgotten that there is another kind of suffering. . .? Can it be possible that you consider the mere pains and privations of the body, and the loss of a paltry sum of money, of a paramount importance to the depression of the mind, and the degradation and pollution of the soul? That the difficulties under which they are laboring, originating from the operation of the State laws, and their absorption by a white population, will affect them in that light, I need not here stop to argue with you. That they have already affected them is a fact too palpable, too notorious for us to deny it. . . . How then can you reconcile your conscience and your sense of what is demanded by the best interest of your people, first with your incessant opposition to *a* treaty, and then your opposition to *the* treaty, because circumstances which had accumulated upon a nation by your delays had compelled, if you please, a minority to make it; and forsooth it does not secure just such a title to the western lands as you may wish; and because a sufficient sum of money is not obtained for the 'invaluable' gold mines, marble quarries, mountains and forests of our country! How can you persist in deluding your people with phantoms, and in your opposition to that which alone is practicable, when you see them dying a moral death.

"To be sure from your account of the condition and circumstances of the Cherokees, the public may form an idea different from what my remarks seem to convey. When applied to a portion of our people, confined mostly to whites intermarried among us, and the descendants of whites, your account [of Cherokee civilization] is probably correct, divesting it of all the exaggeration with which you have encircled it. But look at the mass—look at the entire population as it now is, and say, can you see any indication of a progressing improvement?—anything that can encourage a philanthropist? You know that it is almost a dreary waste. I care not if I am accounted a slanderer of my country's reputation—every observing man in this nation knows that I speak words of truth and soberness. In the light that I consider my countrymen, not as mere animals ... I say their condition is wretched. Look ... around you and see the progress that vice and immorality have already made! See the spread of intemperance and the wretchedness and misery it has already occasioned. I need not reason with a man of your sense and discernment, and of your observation, to show the debasing character of that vice to our people—you will find an argument in every tippling shop in the country—you will find its cruel effects in the bloody tragedies that are frequently occurring—in the frequent convictions and executions for murders, and in the tears and groans of the widows and fatherless, rendered homeless, naked and hungry by this vile curse of our race. ... We are making a rapid tendency to a general immorality and debasement. What more evidence do we need, to prove this general tendency, than the slow but sure insinuation of the lower vices into our female population? Oh, it is heart rending to think of these things, much less speak of them—but the world will know them—the world does know them, and we need not try to hide our shame.

"Now, sir, can you say that in all this the Cherokees had not suffered one half of what their country was worth? Can you presume to be spending your whole time in opposing a treaty, then in trying, as you say, to make a better treaty, that is to get more money, a full compensation for your gold mines, your marble quarries, your forests, your watercourses—I say, can you be doing all this while the canker is eating the very vitals of this nation? Perish your gold mines and your money, if, in pursuit of them, the moral credit of this people, their happiness and their existence are to be sacrificed! ... My language has been, 'fly for your lives'—it is now the same. I would say to my countrymen, you among the rest, fly from the moral pestilence that will finally destroy our nation."[2]

The pamphlet bore little fruit. Although the Cherokees saw approaching the end of the two-year period in which the treaty required them to vacate their mountain country, few took the trail to the West. Ross refused to give up hope that the United States would not force fifteen thousand people to give up their homes against their will. The mass of the Cherokees awaited in despair the word of the Principal Chief.

[2] E. Boudinot, *Letters and Other Papers Relating to Cherokee Affairs.*

23

The Trail of Tears

THE Americans of the first half of the nineteenth century were a humane and freedom-loving people. They were moved by the Greek struggle for independence and they acclaimed the exiled Hungarian patriot, Kossuth. Their fourth of July orators rejoiced that Columbia was a land of refuge for the world's oppressed. And these American forefathers of ours were, without doubt, sincere. But the good people of Cornwall burned Harriet Gold in effigy when she announced her intention to marry a member of another race. In 1838 the United States moved effectively to expel the Cherokees. Except among a few Americans, apparently, sympathy for the underdog did not transcend racial boundaries. The Cherokees, as soon as the Senate had ratified the Treaty of New Echota, confronted conquerors as hard and as terrifying as were ever the Huns of Attila.

General Wool with a detachment of soldiers was ordered to the Cherokee country in May, 1836, to disarm and overawe the Indians and urge them to migrate. The plight of the people touched the commanding officer. He wrote privately to a friend. "The whole scene since I have been in this country has been nothing but a heart rending one. . . . Because I am firm and decided, do not believe I would be unjust. If I could, and I could not do them a greater kindness, I would remove every Indian tomorrow beyond the reach of the white men, who, like vultures, are watching, ready to pounce upon their prey and strip them of everything they have or expect from the government of the United States."[1] In June Major Ridge, now an old man, sent a plea for help to Andrew Jackson. The white people "have got our lands and now they are preparing to fleece us of the money accruing from the treaty. We found our plantations taken either in whole or in part by the Georgians—suits instituted against us for back rents for our own farms. ... Thus our funds will be filched from our people and we shall be compelled to leave our country as beggars and in want. ... The lowest class of white people are flogging the Cherokees with cowhides, hickories, and clubs. We are not safe in our houses—our people are assailed by day and night by the rabble. ... We talk plainly, as chiefs having property and life in danger. ..."[2]

Yet John Ross refused to surrender, and the mass of the nation clung in desperation to their homeland and their leader. The end of the two-year period approached and the Cherokees were still passively resisting. In March, 1838, the Principal Chief was in Washington arguing with the Van Buren administration for a higher price for the Cherokee lands. In the midst of his efforts he paused to read a personal letter from Governor Gilmer of Georgia to himself. The chief executive described the situation bluntly and accurately. "The law of necessity, or, if you please, the harsh and unyielding will of superior power, has determined that the portion of the Cherokees remaining in this

---

[1] Quoted in Mooney, *Myths*, 127.
[2] Ridge to Jackson, June 30, 1836, quoted in Mooney, *Myths*, 127 f.

state, must remove to the country provided for them in the west. How will you meet this necessity against which you can no longer contend?"[3] Ross promptly replied to the governor: "It is my wish to settle all difficulties by amicable treaty, and on perfectly reasonable terms. I sincerely hope that my earnest efforts to that end may ultimately prosper, as one word of the Executive is now enough to save the expense and inevitable danger which must result from the employment of an uncalled-for army. Should blood be spilt, therefore, which I trust can never be the case, the blame can never rest on us."[4]

The defiance was as futile as it was brave. The ink on the letter was scarcely dry when Ross received a call from General Winfield Scott, who had been ordered to the Cherokee country, to remove the Indians, if need be, at the point of the bayonet. The general spoke earnestly. He urged the Principal Chief to bow to the will of the white man and to tell the Cherokees that their cause was lost. The soldier, who knew whereof he spoke, urged the leader, who was more white than red, to save his people from the horrors of a forced removal. John Ross shook his head. He remained in Washington striving for a modification of the treaty. A bitter debate in Congress was in progress at the moment. Northerners were pronouncing philippics against the policy of Georgia. The pious John Schermerhorn read with pain Congressional speeches which described him as a worldly priest who had acquired the distinction of being the most perfidious of all the government agents who had ever dealt with redskins. Talk, however, failed to remove the white

---

[3] Quoted in George R. Gilmer, *Sketches of Some of the First Settlers of Upper Georgia, of the Cherokees, and the Author* (New York, D. Appleton & Co., 1855), 534 f.
[4] *Ibid.*, 537 f.

man's boot from the neck of the Cherokee. Ross returned, defeated, to his tribe.

One of the few Americans who in later generations have interested themselves in the story of the Cherokees was James Mooney, a distinguished pioneer of American anthropology. For four years, from 1887 to 1890, he lived among the Cherokees in what is now Oklahoma collecting myths, legends, and incidents in their history. He sat in the cabins of aged men and women and heard them talk of the days of 1838. He returned to the Qualla reservation in North Carolina and got added details. He even corresponded with such members of the military establishment as he could find. Slowly the picture of the removal of 1838 took shape in his mind. His description remains the classic account of the tragedy.

"Under Scott's orders the troops were disposed at various points throughout the Cherokee country, where stockade forts were erected for gathering in and holding the Indians preparatory to removal. From these, squads of troops were sent to search out with rifle and bayonet every small cabin hidden away in the coves or by the sides of mountain streams, to seize and bring in as prisoners all the occupants however or wherever they might be found. Families at dinner were startled by the sudden gleam of bayonets in the doorway and rose to be driven with blows and oaths along the weary miles of trail that led to the stockade. Men were seized in their fields or going along the road, women were taken from their wheels and children from their play. In many cases, on turning for one last look as they crossed the ridge, they saw their homes in flames, fired by the lawless rabble that followed on the heels of the soldiers to loot and pillage. So keen were these outlaws on the scent that in some instances they were driving off the cattle and other stock of the Indians almost before the soldiers had fairly started their owners in the other direction. Systematic hunts were made by the same men for Indian graves, to rob them of the silver pendants and other valuables deposited with the dead. ... To prevent escape the soldiers had been ordered to approach and surround each house, so far as possible, so as to come upon the occupants without warning. One old patriarch, when thus surprised, calmly called his children and grand-children around him, and, kneeling down, bid them pray with him in their own language, while the astonished soldiers looked on in silence. Then rising he led the way to exile. ...

"All were not thus submissive. One old man Tsali, 'Charley,' was seized with his wife, his brother, his three sons and their families. Exasperated at the brutality accorded his wife, who, being unable to travel fast, was prodded with bayonets to hasten her steps, he urged the other men to join him in a dash for liberty. As he spoke in Cherokee the soldiers, although they heard, understood nothing until each warrior suddenly sprang upon the one nearest and endeavored to wrench his gun from him. The attack was so sudden and unexpected that one soldier was killed and the rest fled, while the Indians escaped to the mountains. Hundreds of others, some of them from the various stockades, managed also to escape to the mountains from time to time, where those who did not die of starvation subsisted on roots and wild berries until the hunt was over. Finding it impracticable to secure these fugitives, General Scott finally tendered them a proposition, through [Colonel] W. H.

Thomas, their most trusted friend, that if they would surrender Charley and his party for punishment, the rest would be allowed to remain until their case could be adjusted by the government. On hearing of the proposition Charley with his sons, offered himself as a sacrifice for his people. By command of General Scott, Charley, his brother, and the two elder sons were shot near the mouth of the Tuckasegee, a detachment of Cherokee prisoners being compelled to do the shooting in order to impress upon the Indians the fact of their utter helplessness. From those fugitives permitted to remain originated the present eastern band of Cherokees."[5]

The hot sun of the southern summer beat down upon the crowded stockades. Rancid bacon and spoiled meal were distributed by avaricious contractors who had covenanted with the government to feed the migrating Indians. The inevitable pestilence appeared. Then John Ross surrendered. His request to be permitted to lead his people into exile was promptly granted. The gates of the stockades were opened and the Indians allowed to live in camps. Life was made more comfortable and disease was checked. John Ross never surpassed the heights which he achieved during those hard months. In the autumn the great body of the Cherokees took what they called "the trail of tears," which led to the country beyond the Mississippi.

June, 1838, found New Echota full of strange faces. On the eighteenth General Charles Floyd of the Georgia militia stood in the midst of the old capital of the Cherokees and looked about him with satisfaction. There was the abandoned council house. Not far away was the habitation

[5] Mooney, *Myths*, 130 f.

which had been the home of Harriet Boudinot. Her grave was only a few paces distant. General Floyd walked into the "Head Quarters" of the "Middle Military District" and wrote a letter to his chief, Governor Gilmer. "I have the pleasure to inform your excellency that I am now fully convinced there is not an Indian within the limits of my command, except a few in my possession, who will be sent to Ross' Landing to-morrow. My scouting parties have scoured the whole country without seeing an Indian, or late Indian signs. If there are any stragglers in Georgia, they must be in Union and Gilmer counties, and near the Tennessee and North Carolina line; but none can escape the vigilance of our troops. Georgia is ultimately in possession of her rights in the Cherokee country."[6]

[6] *Army and Navy Chronicle*, VII, 57. Quoted in Grant Foreman, *Indian Removal* (Norman, University of Oklahoma Press, 1932), 296. Foreman's is a fine and full account of the Cherokee removal.

PART IV
THE WEST

24

The Darkening Land

IN 1835 Samuel and Ann Worcester took up their work in the country of the western Cherokees. Samuel promptly established a church and a school. Single-handed he resumed the old task of translating the Bible into the Cherokee tongue. He worked also at a Cherokee dictionary and grammar, indispensable tools for other translators. He was handicapped by the absence of Elias Boudinot. In the midst of his labors he received word that his old friend had put his name to the fateful Treaty of New Echota.

Worcester disapproved on moral grounds of the treaty and of his colleague's part in its formulation. But the missionary had no intention of permitting his scruples to destroy a long and intimate friendship. He needed Boudinot, moreover, in his work. So it came about that Worcester unexpectedly found himself in the position of defending his colleague and friend to the missionary brethren at Boston, who also questioned the ethics of the New Echota Treaty. "The feeling of the Cherokees against Boudinot," Worcester explained in 1838 to the A.B.C.F.M., "is founded on interest, or supposed interest, and not on principle. It is not because he has done what is morally wrong, that they are excited against him. And very much of that excitement will be allayed . . . when they find themselves undeceived as to what Mr. Ross can do for them, and as to the character of the country to which they are sent. The late emigrants have almost universally, so far as I have known, expressed great surprise on their arrival, or soon after, at the goodness of the country. Nothing is more common than the remark, 'This is a far better country than I supposed I was coming to'—'This is a very different country from what our leading men have told us'. . . . And this discovery will of necessity affect the feelings of the people toward Mr. Boudinot. They will consider themselves as having been in this respect grossly deceived by Mr. Ross." Worcester added that in his opinion the treaty was a "fraudulent and wicked transaction . . . while I still believe that Mr. Boudinot was, in the ordinary sense of the term, conscientious in the part he acted."[1]

The Boston men were convinced. The spring of 1839 found Elias Boudinot in Park Hill, busy with the task which had been begun so many years before. With him was his wife, Delight Sargent, a white woman whom Elias had long known as a member, with the Samuel Worcesters, of the missionary band working among the Cherokees. She was mother to Harriet's orphaned children. Boudinot was impoverished, and Worcester had to request the Board for five hundred dollars with which to build a house for his friend. The migration of the eastern Cherokees was completed and they were already becoming familiar with their new home. Winter was giving way to spring. Worcester's Park Hill letters to Boston were full of enthusiasm.

Samuel Worcester, however, in spite of his years of labor among the Cherokees, had not yet learned the depths of Indian character. He thought that time would heal the wounds of 1838. As he hurried, full of hope, from task to

---

[1] Worcester to D. Greene, June 28, 1838, in *Worcester Mss.*, Andover.

task three hundred untutored full bloods were organizing themselves into a secret band. Each member had suffered in the expulsion and migration the loss of wife or relative. They were not civilized—they disdained the white man's culture. They were Indians who could not and would not forget the suffering which the conqueror had brought upon them. But the white man was far away, fattening in the country where their fathers were buried. They could not strike back at the victor. But in their midst still lived the three signers of the treaty the defiance of which had brought the white man's bayonets among them. Secretly the three hundred invoked the ancient law of vengeance. They kept their plot from John Ross, for they were sure that he would disapprove and would attempt to balk them. In the darkness of the night on June 22, 1839, one party dragged John Ridge from his house and killed him. Another ambushed Major Ridge and left him dead by the road side.

Samuel Worcester, with a heavy heart, described to Boston the doings of a third group. "Mr. Boudinot was yet living at my house. On Saturday morning he went to his house, which he was building a quarter of a mile distant. There some Cherokee men came up, inquiring for medicine, and Mr. Boudinot set out with two of them to get it. He had walked but a few rods when his shriek was heard by his hired men, who ran to his help; but before they could come the deed was done. A stab in the back with a knife, and seven gashes in the head with a hatchet, did the bloody work. . . . The murderers ran a short distance into the woods, joined a company of armed men on horse back, and made their escape. . . . He had fallen a victim . . . to his honest . . . zeal for the preservation of his people. In his own view he risked his life to save his people from ruin, and he realized his fears."[2]

[2] Worcester to D. Greene, June 26, 1839, in *Worcester Mss.*

After his death, Delight Sargent Boudinot took her husband's children to New England, where they were all educated. General D. B. Brinsmade and his wife acted as their guardians while the children were in the North. They did not all live with the general and his wife, however. Some of them lived in Vermont. One son, William Penn, became a successful engraver in Philadelphia, while Elias Cornelius studied civil engineering in Vermont. Both later removed to the West, where they engaged in much important public service for the Cherokee Nation. Elias Cornelius was for a time an officer in the Cherokee detachment of the Confederate army commanded by his uncle, General Stand Watie, but his greatest importance rests upon his service as delegate from the Cherokee Nation to the Confederate Congress at Richmond. Frank Boudinot did not return to Indian Territory. Having enlisted in the Union army, he was fatally wounded in one of the last battles before Richmond. Eleanor studied in the North and later was married to Henry J. Church. Mary, after attending Mount Holyoke College, was married to Lyman Case. Sarah died as a girl. See Dale and Litton, *Cherokee Cavaliers*.

APPENDIX

Appendix

THE story of the Cornwall Mission School became part of the local history of this township in the northwestern part of Connecticut. The large tombstone that still marks Obookiah's grave continues to remind new generations of the strange episode associated with the name of the Hawaiian boy. John Warner Barber in his since famous *Connecticut Historical Collections* (1838) set down a brief account both of the school and of Obookiah. But he did not mention the Indian marriages and made no effort to explain the closing of the institution. The story of the marriages was preserved in the form of oral tradition partly within the families concerned and partly as a tradition of the locality. It was almost a legend, the recollection of an event that had happened but about which little was known. Some of the details of the Ridge-Northrup marriage were preserved in the narrative poem printed below. The date of the writing is not known but was apparently near the event and was probably before the marriage of Harriet Gold and Elias Boudinot. That alliance is not mentioned in it. If Barber knew about these verses, he suppressed them. Theodore S. Gold recovered them in 1877 and, so far as is known, published them for the first time. He included them in his *History of Cornwall, Connecticut* (1877). He stated that he knew several people who remembered having read them.

The verses were, therefore, part of the folklore of Cornwall. As folklore they occupy a middle position between oral legend and the ballad that is sung. They undoubtedly aided materially in keeping alive a partially fictionized version of the marriage. They are in fact, a ballad that for some reason never reached full maturity. They are reprinted here as a contribution to American folklore.

The Indian Song, Sarah and John

BY EMILY FOX OF CORNWALL[1]

Behold, there came into our town,
A man of fame and great renown;
He had thought to live in splendor here,
And brought with him a daughter dear.

She was blest with beauty bright and fair,
There were few with her could compare.
O, 'tis hard for to relate the truth,
She fell in love with an Indian youth!

He was a bright young man, we know,
And with him she resolved to go.
He flattered her to be his young dove,
Till her young heart was filled with love.

Then to her mother he did go,
To see whether he might have her or no.
She was well pleas'd at the words of John,
And consented that he should be her son.

They kept it a secret, and did not tell,
How Sarah loved an Indian well;
Nor was the secret thing made known,
Till from his country he did return.

---

[1] From *History of Cornwall, Connecticut*, collected and arranged by Theodore S. Gold, 1877, pages 32-34.

Her father then being out of town,
And when he heard that John had come,
He sighed, and for his child did mourn,
Saying, O that my Sarah had not been born.

And when this Indian he had come,
She thought her daughter was undone;
She made as though her heart would break,
And it was for her daughter's sake.

She being then borne down with grief,
Went to her neighbor for relief,
Saying, my sorrows, friend, are hard to tell;
Our Sarah loves this Indian well.

What shall I do, what can I say;
Can I bear my child should go away?
For she is young and in her bloom,—
We'll fasten her tight in a room.

O fasten her, I think to say;
She with the Indian shall not stay;
Then in distraction this fair maid did run,
It was for the love of an Indian man.

Declaring if she was not his wife,
Most suddenly she would end her life.
Sickness on her then did fall,
And for the doctor they did call.

He gave them soon to understand,
'Twas for the love of an Indian man.
Unto her parents he did tell,
Let her have him and she will be well.

The Reverend Vaill we would not blame;
On Sabbath next he published them,
But Reverend Smith feared not the law,
He married this lady to be a squaw.

Highly promoted were Sarah and John,
Col. Gold did them wait upon,
He waited on them most genteel too,
And seated them in his own pew.

Upon her side it does look dark,
To think how she used her neighbor Clark—
Has left behind for to make sport,
To think she did with an Indian court.

He went with her both night and day,
While her dear John was gone away.
And unto him she did not tell
How that she loved an Indian well.

He being absent from his friends,
A letter unto her he did send,
And unto it she would not hear,
But married John her only dear.

Her parents with her a piece did go,
To bid their lovely child adieu—
Now with her mother she must part,
Which was enough to break her heart.

She hung upon her mother's breast,
With sighs and tears did her embrace,
I can not bear, I am sure, said she,
My tender mother, to leave thee.

He snatch'd her from the mother's breast,
And his tawny arms did her embrace,
Sarah, said he, you are mine you know,
And with me you have got to go.

Now Sarah is gone and seen no more—
She has gone and left her native shore—
Ah! yes, she has gone but proved unkind,
And left her whole disgrace behind.

She thinks great splendor she shall see,
When she arrives at Cherokee—
She thinks great splendor there is seen,
And she be crowned for a queen.

She would be disappointed of her home,
To find a little, small wigwam,
And nothing allowed her for a bed,
But a dirty blanket, it is said.

And this be hard for Sarah fair,
Who long did live in splendor here,
To lay aside her laces and fine gowns,
Her Indian blanket to put on.

'Twould sink her pride—'twould raise her shame
To follow him and carry game,
And with her John must march along,
Amidst a savage whooping throng.

Come all young maids I pray take care
How Indians draw you into a snare,
For if they do I fear it will be
As it is with our fair Sarah.

*And what a dreadful, doleful sound
Is often heard from town to town,
Reflecting words from every friend,
How our ladies marry Indian men.*

*Now Sarah is gone—her we ne'er shall view—
She's gone, and to her love proves true,
O yes, she's gone, and her Indian too—
Now Sarah we will bid adieu.*

INDEX

Index

ADAIR, James, 10-14, 19, 21
American Board of Commissioners for Foreign Missions, 95 f., 175-78
Andover Theological Seminary, 4 f., 39

"BACHELORS of Cornwall Valley," 63 f.
Bartram, William, 5-10, 19
Beecher, Lyman, 62, 77, 91, 132
Bloody Fellow, 23
Boot, 23
Boudinot, Eleanor, 112, 119, 178
Boudinot, Elias (Cherokee), childhood, 4; at Spring Place, 30; comes to Cornwall, 30, 33 f., 52-55; marriage, 70 f., 76 f., 82, 86, 90-92; at Philadelphia, 3, 34; at High Tower, 97-100, 103; editor, 111-19, 120 f., 123-26, 128, 129 f., 132 f., 134; favors removal, 139 f.; at Red Clay, 142-45; and Treaty of New Echota, 148-55; describes death of wife, 157; argues for removal, 159-64; death, 175-78
Boudinot, Elias (philanthropist), 3
Boudinot, Elias Cornelius, 178
Boudinot, Frank, 178
Boudinot, Harriet Gold, 65-98, 111 f., 119, 156-58
Boudinot, Mary, 112, 119, 178
Boudinot, Sarah, 178
Boudinot, William Penn, 112, 119, 178
Brainerd Mission, 98, 100
Brinsmade, Daniel B., 66, 74 f., 81, 178
Brinsmade, Mary, 66, 68 f., 85, 89 f.
Brown, David, 53
Bunce, Isaiah, 57-65

CASS, Lewis, 144, 147, 151 f.
Cherokee Phœnix, 109 f., 112-14, 123-28, 133, 134, 139
Cherokees, and American Revolution, 19 f.; culture (primitive), 4-18; culture (in transition), 106-08, 112, 121-24, 137 f., 161-64; constitution, 122; dances, 8-10, 12-14; homeland, 5; importance of mixed bloods, 138; myths, 5 f., 15-19; removal, 165-71
Clingman's Dome, 5
Coosawatee, 24
Cornwall, 30, 33 f., 40, 43 f., 49-51, 66-80
Cowe, 8, 19
Creeks, 20, 136
Curry, B. F., 145

DAGGETT, Herman, 50-55, 62
Deism, 19, 37
Doublehead, 23
Dwight, Timothy, 3, 19, 37, 40 f., 46

ECHOTA, 11
Edwards, Jonathan, 3, 19, 50
Enlightenment, 3
Evarts, Jeremiah, 99, 120, 123
Everest, Cornelius B., 66, 86 f.
Everett, Edward, 126 f.

FLOYD, Charles, 170 f.
Foreign Mission School, 40-42, 43, 45, 49-56, 82 f., 91

GAMBOLD, Anna, 22, 28-30, 95
Gambold, John, 22, 25-28, 95, 98, 145
Georgia, and the Cherokees, 120-33, 139 f., 141 f., 150 f., 170 f.
Gilmer, George R., 166 f.
Gold, Benjamin, 43-46, 54-56, 57, 64 f., 66-72, 82, 87-92, 115-19
Gold, Catherine, 86
Gold, Eleanor, 67-77, 82
Gold, Hezekiah, 45 f.
Gold, Ruggles, 47
Great Smokies, 5

HARVEY, Joseph, 49, 62, 75-77, 82, 91
Hicks, Charles, 24, 28
Hicks, Elijah, 134
High Tower, 96-100
Hodgson, Adam, 54-56

Jackson, Andrew, 127, 133, 136, 155, 166

Lewis, John C., 63, 78
Little Turkey, 23

Marshall, John, 131, 133
Mayas, 19
Meigs, John, 135
Meigs, Lewis, 135
Meigs, Return Jonathan, 135
Mooney, James, 167-70
Moravian Mission, 22-30, 141 f.

New Echota, 109-19, 170 f.
New Haven, 35-37, 60
Northrup, Sarah B., 61 f., 182-86

Obookiah, 33-42
Oostanaula, 24

Payne, John Howard, 150
Payne, Rufus, 63, 78
Philadelphia, 3 f.
Prentice, Charles, 62

Qualla Reservation, 168

Rabbit Trap, 24
Red Clay, 141-47
Ridge, John, 60-62, 139 f., 144-46, 148-55, 177, 182-86
Ridge, Major, 139 f., 144-46, 166, 177
Ross, John, 134-40, 144-47, 148-52, 159-64, 166-68, 170, 176, 177
Ross, Lewis, 115, 116, 135
Ross's Landing, 136

Sargent, Delight, 176
Schermerhorn, John F., 145 f., 152-55, 167
Scott, Winfield, 167-70
Sequoyah, 100-05, 124, 125
Spring Place, 22-30, 95, 112, 141 f.
Stone, Mary, 39 f., 47, 80, 81, 82
Stone, Timothy, 36, 39 f., 46-48, 52, 62, 75, 77, 81, 91
Sumac Town, 24
Swift, Philo, 77

Tecumseh, 136
Tellico, 23
Thomas, W. H., 169 f.
Torringford (Torrington), 37 f.
Treadwell, John, 49
Treaty of New Echota, 148-55, 165-67, 175
Tsali ("Charley"), 169

Unakas, 5

Vaill, Herman, 51-53, 79, 81, 82-85, 86-88, 90 f., 118
Vann, James, 24-26
Vann's Place, 24-26

Watie, Stand, 96, 132, 178
Wool, General, 165-70
Worcester, Ann Orr, 98, 112, 130 f., 157, 175
Worcester, Samuel Austin, 98-100, 112-14, 124, 140, 145, 175-78

Yale College, 36 f., 46

ELIAS BOUDINOT, CHEROKEE
AND HIS AMERICA
BY RALPH HENRY GABRIEL
HAS BEEN COMPOSED ON THE
LINOTYPE IN TWELVE POINT GRANJON
THE PAPER IS ANTIQUE WOVE

UNIVERSITY OF OKLAHOMA PRESS
NORMAN, OKLAHOMA

www.ingramcontent.com/pod-product-compliance
Lightning Source LLC
Chambersburg PA
CBHW020838160426
43192CB00007B/703